# Teacher's Guide
# to Effective Sentence Writing

# WHAT WORKS FOR SPECIAL-NEEDS LEARNERS

Karen R. Harris and Steve Graham
*Editors*

Strategy Instruction for Students with Learning Disabilities
*Robert Reid and Torri Ortiz Lienemann*

Teaching Mathematics to Middle School Students
with Learning Difficulties
*Marjorie Montague and Asha K. Jitendra, Editors*

Teaching Word Recognition:
Effective Strategies for Students with Learning Difficulties
*Rollanda E. O'Connor*

Teaching Reading Comprehension to Students
with Learning Difficulties
*Janette K. Klingner, Sharon Vaughn, and Alison Boardman*

Promoting Self-Determination in Students
with Developmental Disabilities
*Michael L. Wehmeyer with Martin Agran, Carolyn Hughes,
James E. Martin, Dennis E. Mithaug, and Susan B. Palmer*

Instructional Practices for Students with Behavioral Disorders:
Strategies for Reading, Writing, and Math
*J. Ron Nelson, Gregory J. Benner, and Paul Mooney*

Working with Families of Young Children
with Special Needs
*R. A. McWilliam, Editor*

Promoting Executive Function in the Classroom
*Lynn Meltzer*

Managing Challenging Behaviors in Schools:
Research-Based Strategies That Work
*Kathleen Lynne Lane, Holly Mariah Menzies, Allison L. Bruhn,
and Mary Crnobori*

Explicit Instruction: Effective and Efficient Teaching
*Anita L. Archer and Charles A. Hughes*

Teacher's Guide to ADHD
*Robert Reid and Joseph Johnson*

Vocabulary Instruction for Struggling Students
*Patricia F. Vadasy and J. Ron Nelson*

Preparing Effective Special Education Teachers
*Nancy Mamlin*

RTI for Reading at the Secondary Level:
Recommended Literacy Practices and Remaining Questions
*Deborah K. Reed, Jade Wexler, and Sharon Vaughn*

Inclusive Instruction:
Evidence-Based Practices for Teaching Students with Disabilities
*Mary T. Brownell, Sean J. Smith, Jean B. Crockett, and Cynthia C. Griffin*

Universal Design for Learning in the Classroom:
Practical Applications
*Tracey E. Hall, Anne Meyer, and David H. Rose, Editors*

Teacher's Guide to Effective Sentence Writing
*Bruce Saddler*

# Teacher's Guide to Effective Sentence Writing

Bruce Saddler

THE GUILFORD PRESS
New York    London

© 2012 The Guilford Press
A Division of Guilford Publications, Inc.
370 Seventh Avenue, Suite 1200, New York, NY 10001
www.guilford.com

Printed in the United States of America

This book is printed on acid-free paper.

Last digit is print number:   9   8   7   6   5   4   3

**Library of Congress Cataloging-in-Publication Data**

Saddler, Bruce.
   Teacher's guide to effective sentence writing / Bruce Saddler.
      p. cm. — (What works for special-needs learners)
   Includes bibliographical references and index.
   ISBN 978-1-4625-0677-4 (pbk.: alk. paper) — ISBN 978-1-4625-0682-8
(hardcover : alk. paper)
   1. English language—Sentences—Study and teaching.   2. English language—
Composition and exercises—Study and teaching.   3. Learning disabled children—
Education.   I. Title.
   LB1576.S228 2012
   808'.042071—dc23
                                                                    2012025799

# About the Author

**Bruce Saddler, PhD,** is Associate Professor in the Division of Special Education at the University at Albany, State University of New York. A former K–12 special education teacher and teacher of the year, he conducts and publishes empirical research and provides professional workshops on writing and the remediation of writing difficulties. He has received numerous grants to fund his research and has published over 40 articles in many prestigious journals; he has also conducted over 80 presentations, workshops, and clinics throughout the United States and Canada. Of particular interest to Dr. Saddler is sentence combining, a writing technique he has spent over a decade investigating, teaching, and discussing.

# Preface

My purpose for *Teacher's Guide to Effective Sentence Writing* is to help educators teach students with and without disabilities the critical writing skill of sentence construction through sentence-combining activities. This book represents the knowledge I have gleaned from a decade's worth of studying, teaching, and researching sentence combining. The information included in this book will help you understand how important sentence construction skills are to a writer and how to incorporate sentence-level instruction into a writing process approach.

Sentence combining is a fun, playful approach to language that will help writers experiment with different ways to arrange thoughts. I have designed the book to be as comprehensive as possible, to allow you to begin using sentence combining right away. Throughout the book, you will find theory, practical information, and a sequential series of model exercises. I have also included many practice activities, because I believe you will better understand sentence combining by first trying out what you will eventually teach to your students. Approach these practice activities as though they were a game, and have fun with expressing your ideas in a variety of ways.

I have organized this volume into three main sections: Part I: Background; Part II: Teaching and Assessment; and Part III: Sample Unit of Instruction, Practice Activities, and Exercises. In Part I you will find a brief overview of the benefits and challenges of writing, especially for children with disabilities. I then discuss why sentence-level skills are so important to learn, and I explain sentence combining. Part II provides directions for teaching sentence-combining and sentence-creating exercises, as well as a chapter devoted specifically to assessing student progress. Part III begins with a model unit of instruction, and then provides several practice activities to help students extend and generalize their skills. It continues with a suggested sequence of sentence-combining skills, as well as a number of exercise examples suitable for various grade levels. The exercises begin with word insertions and proceed to phrase-, clause-, and paragraph-length problems.

I sincerely hope that you find sentence combining as intriguing as I do, and that this book helps you to help your students write more effectively.

# Acknowledgments

I am indebted to the constant encouragement and support of two people: my wife and colleague, Kristie, and my friend and mentor Steve Graham. Thank you both for believing in me and challenging me. This book would not have been possible without each of you in my life.

# Contents

## PART III.  SAMPLE UNIT OF INSTRUCTION, PRACTICE ACTIVITIES, AND EXERCISES

# PART I

BACKGROUND

CHAPTER 1

# Writing Basics

If there is one absolute truth in writing, it's that writing can be absolutely difficult to teach and to learn. Although writing can be wonderfully creative, it is also a maddening, frustrating, highly complex activity that includes many components or processes a writer must navigate and many decisions the writer must make before a piece is completed.

Not surprisingly, many students struggle with writing (Graham & Perin, 2007; Schumaker & Deschler, 2009). And although writing can be difficult for students of average or even above-average academic achievement, it can present a significant challenge for students who struggle with writing or who have documented writing disabilities (Graham, 2006; Kame'enui & Simmons, 1990; Mason & Graham, 2008). Children with writing difficulties/disabilities can exhibit very different characteristics from skilled writers and may have difficulties with all aspects of writing (Troia, 2006). For example, they may not engage in effective planning prior to writing (Baker, Gersten, & Graham, 2003). They may also write very brief papers that are not well organized or cohesive, and these papers may lack important details or elaborations that could make them more enjoyable or understandable to readers (Wong, Graham, Hoskyn, & Berman, 2008). Sadly, the students usually cannot improve their papers through revising, as they often fail to make meaning-improving revisions (Graham, 2006; MacArthur, 2007; Nodine, Barenbaum, & Newcomer, 1985). They may also struggle with other components of writing, including handwriting, grammar, punctuation, and spelling. Furthermore, they may lack awareness of audience needs or of genre requirements and forms (Newcomer, Nodine, & Barenbaum, 1988; Wong, Wong, Darlington, & Jones, 1991). Perhaps because of the struggles they face while writing, many children with writing difficulties/disabilities may have less positive images of their writing and their ability as writers (Graham & Harris, 1989).

Although writing effectively can be very difficult, it is an important skill to learn (Mason & Graham, 2008). Teachers often use writing as a primary means to document student knowledge and a major instrument to evaluate academic performance (Graham & Harris, 2004; MacArthur & Philippakos, 2010). In addition, the growing emphasis on writing in federal- and state-mandated accountability testing and college entrance examinations means teachers must ensure that all students achieve some level of competence with the required writing components (Schumaker & Deschler, 2009). Moreover, writing is a key means of communication, and good communication skills are essential in many areas of life after school; many jobs, for example, require facility in basic written language. Finally, aside from the practical advantages of knowing how to write effectively, writing well can also allow people to explore, organize, and refine their thoughts (Applebee, 1984) and to describe to others what they are remembering, feeling, seeing, experiencing, or wanting through a visible and durable method.

## THE WRITING PROCESS

Generally, to represent and transmit their thoughts effectively, writers proceed through several stages or steps. They will probably first think about or plan (at least in general terms) what they want to say. They may then begin to write down or draft their ideas into an organized format, allowing them to "see" their thoughts. Revision usually follows as the writers grind closer to a final version that most closely matches what they really want to say. While engaged in these processes, the writers must also consider such tasks as how to spell challenging words, which words need capitalization, and how to apply punctuation accurately.

Seldom does a writer plan, draft, and revise a piece of text straight through from beginning to end. Instead, the writer often encounters some difficulties or decision points—for example, "What do I want to say next? How does this next thought fit in with what I have written?" or "Which word might better convey my thought?" Often there may be multiple solutions to these difficulties (e.g., "Several words would work, but which is the best?"). In these situations, which can occur frequently, the writer must test new ideas for suitability as the meaning he or she is trying to convey unfolds. The testing of ideas may require a reread before additional text is created. However, the new solution may force a revision of the initial plan or the section of text just written. Additional text may then be generated based on the revised plan, and the new information may be united to the existing through a short round of revision to make sure the document reads well. This complex, messy, fluid, dynamic, recursive, and sometimes frustrating process places writers in a continual state of creation, consideration, and revision, in which they must solve the problems a writing task may present on their way to creating understandable language that matches their knowledge of a topic or their thoughts and feelings (Berninger, 1993).

Teaching writers to navigate the processes of writing is understandably challenging, given the available options. How best to teach writing is debatable, and although specific techniques have been empirically proven to be effective, no single technique will work for all writers.

In the next chapter I discuss a foundational component of writing: the sentence.

# CHAPTER 2

## The Importance of the Sentence

The process of writing places many demands on every writer, as planning, drafting, and revising all require considerable cognitive effort. However, of all these writing components and processes, creating sentences may be the most complex.

The late historian Barbara Tuchman once wrote, "When it comes to language, nothing is more satisfying than to write a good sentence" (quoted in Beene, 1996, p. 7). Sentences represent vehicles of communication that are literally miniature compositions. When writers produce sentences, they are converting their mental ideas and intentions into syntactically acceptable written forms capable of transmitting particular messages to readers.

Sentences ideally appear during the initial draft of a piece of writing, after the author has created a basic written plan. The plan may be only short snippets of information in either single-word or phrase format, but the writer must convert these into sentences that eventually support and build on each other. Hayes and Flower (1987) suggest that the process of initial planning through sentence generation involves three steps; first explaining briefly sketched ideas (i.e., "the big issues"), then interpreting nonverbal material in verbal form (e.g., "Just how did he look?"), and finally carrying out instructions (e.g., "Write a catchy introduction").

### SENTENCE VARIATIONS

Depending on a writer's choices, intent, and ability, a composition can contain an extensive variety of syntactically different sentences—some shorter and some longer; some designed to inform or command; others intended to convey emotions, make a statement, or pose questions. For example, a writer can use a short sentence for emphasizing a critical point or for simple dialogue, and then slip in a more complex sentence construction to elaborate a key concept or plot twist. Writers can also repeat certain elements within a series of sentences for a specific effect. Whatever the length may be, however, each sentence will ideally make a unique and identifiable contribution to the whole.

Although sentence variation is a very good thing, teaching writers to make *effective* choices when considering how to represent an idea within the confines of a sentence is difficult, as unfortunately there are no rules for what sentence might work best in a given rhetorical situation. "Best" is related to how an author desires to represent an idea, and how an idea is represented relates directly to the *style* of the author. In writing, "style" is the total impact of a writer's words, sentence structures, details, images, and rhetorical patterns. It is literally a "way with words" (Neman, 1995). The style in which a writer expresses thoughts can have a powerful effect on a reader (Butler, 2011).

"Style" is often found as part of state standards for writing; it is sometimes stated there as a student's ability to use standard English skillfully and in an individual manner. For example, the New York State Learning Standards in English language arts require students to "produce clear and coherent writing in which the development, organization, and style are appropriate to task, purpose, and audience."[1] Style is included in Oregon's standards as well, with "good" writing defined as "a writing style that is lively and interesting and is appropriate to the audience and topic. Sentences that are smooth, varied, and carefully constructed."[2] Finally, writing standards in Wisconsin encourage students to "write for a variety of readers, including peers, teachers, and other adults, adapting content, style, and structure to audience and situation."[3]

Although it is certainly an important skill, developing a style in writing is a complex business to teach and learn, in part because of the variety of sentences that can be used. Guidance is available, however. One of the seminal books on developing writing, *The Elements of Style* (Strunk & White, 1979), provides this description of an effective sentence:

> A sentence should contain no unnecessary words, a paragraph no unnecessary sentences for the same reason a drawing should have no unnecessary lines and a machine no unnecessary parts. This requires not that the writer make all his sentences short, or that he avoid all detail and treat his subjects only in outline, but that every word tell [something important]. . . . (p. 23)

---

[1] *www.p12.nysed.gov/ciai/common_core_standards/pdfdocs/p12_ common_core_learning_standards_ ela_final.pdf*

[2] *www.ode.state.or.us/teachlearn/subjects/elarts/goodwritingtraits.pdf*

[3] *http://dpi.wi.gov/standards/elab8.html*

According to Strunk and White's description, then, making each word add something important to the meaning conveyed in a sentence is a goal for every writer to work toward. By choosing words within each sentence that contribute precisely and clearly to this meaning, the writer makes the composition more understandable to the reader. And then by placing those words within a variety of sentences, the writer can create a unique rhythm and flow that make reading the composition easier and more enjoyable. However, deciding which words to put into a specific type of sentence can test the ability of any writer; indeed, according to Henry David Thoreau, is a singular event when it does occur:

> A perfectly healthy sentence, it is true, is extremely rare. For the most part we miss the hue and fragrance of the thought; as if we could be satisfied with the dews of the morning or evening without their colors, or the heavens without their azure. (Quoted in "A Perfectly Healthy Sentence," n.d.)

## THE FIRST SENTENCES

Young writers usually begin learning how to generate sentences by creating simple, or "kernel," sentences that may mirror the sentences they are exposed to in their readings. For example, a first grader may produce the following story:

### A Scary Time

The boy ran. The dog barked. The boy stopped.

There is a degree of safety for young writers within the confines of a basic noun–verb sentence structure. These structures are familiar. They are relatively easy to teach and produce. They can be readily changed by swapping words. Structures such as these are quite common in the work of even skilled writers, but the difference is that skilled writers do not use such constructions exclusively. Young writers must quickly add other sentence structures to their repertoires, because too many simple sentences may make a story less desirable to read, as in this example:

### A Boring Tale

The sentences were short. The sentences were simple. The story became dull.

Luckily, it seems that students will move away from these simple sentences and begin to create longer and more syntactically intricate structures as they mature. Hunt (1965), for example, noted that sentence length increased in samples produced by writers ranging from grade 4 students to skilled adults (see Table 2.1).

**TABLE 2.1. Sentence-Length Increases at Four Levels**

| Level | Number of words per sentence |
|---|---|
| Grade 4 | 13 |
| Grade 8 | 16 |
| Grade 12 | 17 |
| Adult | 25 |

## SYNTACTIC CONTROL

Theoretically, these increases in sentence sophistication may occur as students begin to read more complex material, or perhaps through exposure to more complex syntactic structures during writing instruction. Whatever the influence is, though, creating these longer and more syntactically intricate structures requires a high level of "syntactic control"—that is, the ability to create a variety of sentences that clearly express an intended meaning.

There are several compelling reasons why learning to control syntax is important for young writers:

• Sentence generation (along with planning and revising) is considered a critical component of the writing process (Hayes & Flower, 1986). It is a vital aspect of the initial creation of text in writing, because a writer needs to know not only what to say, but how to say it best (O'Hare, 1973).

• Problems with sentence production skills may interfere with other writing processes, such as planning, content generation, and revising. The attention a writer may need to devote to such skills as the grammatical structuring of language may drain the available cognitive resources in working memory, which otherwise could be applied to such tasks as audience needs and overall goals (Graham, 1997; Scardamalia & Bereiter, 1986; Strong, 1986).

• Lack of knowledge of effective writing structures at the sentence level hampers a writer's ability to convert thoughts from unwritten ideas or brief notes into text (Hayes & Flower, 1986), and thus affects the complexity and coherence of the communication (Berninger, Nagy, & Beers, 2011).

• Difficulties in constructing effective, grammatically acceptable sentences may make the material written by students tricky for others to read. Poorly written sentences may also mean lower scores on written products for such students, because sentence structure has a strong influence on the quality of students' texts.

## SYNTACTIC CONTROL DIFFICULTIES

Although learning to control syntax is an essential skill for all writers, not all writers will develop this skill at the same pace. For some writers, especially writers with disabilities, this process may develop very slowly; in fact, the difference between the syntactic control of writers with and without disabilities appears to increase with age (Andolina, 1980). What this means in practical terms is that as written language becomes more important to school success and more syntactically complex, the syntactic maturity of the writings of children with disabilities remains very simple (Morris & Crump, 1982). Their compositions are often filled with short, simple sentences that sound very similar to one another (Myklebust, 1973; Morris & Crump, 1982; Houck & Billingsley, 1989). In these sentences words may be omitted or placed incorrectly; verbs, pronouns, and word endings (e.g., singular form instead of plural) may be faulty; and the connector *and* may be overused while the children are attempting to create more complex sentences (Anderson, 1982; Englert & Raphael, 1988; Morris & Crump, 1982). Wordiness, ambiguity, ineffective word choice, passive voice, unnecessary repetition, and hyperbole may also be problematic. Unfortunately, time, maturation, and typical school interventions often fail to help these children improve (Christenson, Thurlow, Ysseldyke, & McVicar, 1989; Newcomer & Barenbaum, 1991).

The importance of leaning syntactic control means that all writers, but especially less skilled writers and writers with disabilities, need to develop skill in structuring text within a variety of sentence formats. Because syntactic control is a difficult skill to learn for many writers, any increase in ability may only occur through direct instruction methods (Martlew, 1983) that include deliberate, stimulating language experiences geared toward "cognitively nudging" or accelerating the natural development of syntactic patterns throughout the school years. This direct method may be a kind of sentence-building program designed to increase young writers' ability to manipulate syntax by providing systematic and purposeful practice in such manipulations. Sentence combining, as described in this book, is exactly the type of sentence-building program needed to provide direct instruction in sentence-level skills.

In the next chapter I explain the origins, theory, and practical benefits of sentence combining.

CHAPTER 3

# What Is Sentence Combining?

A sentence-building program is certainly not a new idea in education. In fact, since the mid-1960s researchers have encouraged schools to help students learn to write more syntactically mature sentences. For example, in his preface to the seminal Hunt (1965) study, Carlsen declared that schools should facilitate students' moving in the direction of mature writing patterns. In the years since Carlsen's statement, one method has received a significant amount of interest from researchers: "sentence combining," hereafter referred to in the text as SC for short.

## SENTENCE-COMBINING BASICS

A typical beginning SC practice exercise would present the writer with simple sentences that need to be changed into one longer, more syntactically complex sentence, as depicted below.

**Problem:**  The book was long.
The book was interesting.

**Solution:**  The book was long and interesting.

Conceptually, SC practice such as this was originally based on theories of grammar conceived by Noam Chomsky (1957). Chomsky attempted to demystify the construction of language by explaining how users can create complex sentences from just a few basic (or "kernel") sentence patterns. "Kernel" sentences are very simple sentences that are the spoken or written expressions of a writer's basic thoughts. Chomsky believed that typical sentences in written texts consist of many basic kernels, each adding to the general gist of the text. In the English language, a kernel sentence is a simple sentence (S) consisting of a subject (NP) and a predicate (VP). In mathematical terms, this arrangement could be represented as

$$S = NP + VP$$

The assumption in SC practice, as in Chomsky's theories, is that all the sentences we actually speak or write are derived from these same simple basic sentence units. According to SC/Chomskyan theory, our minds combine these kernel sentences in a myriad of ways to create any number of possible sentences (Frank, 1993).

For example, this sentence from *Frankenstein*—"I quitted my seat, and walked on, although the darkness and storm increased every minute, and the thunder burst with a terrific crash over my head" (Shelley, 1818/2003, p. 68)—represents ideas that perhaps began in Mary Shelley's mind in the form of kernels such as those depicted below.

I quitted my seat.
I walked on.
The darkness increased.
The storm increased.
The increase was by the minute.
The thunder burst.
It burst with a crash.
The crash was terrific.
The thunder was over my head.

Interestingly, these kernels could be transformed in many ways, two of which are depicted below.

**Solution 1:** With the darkness and storm increasing every minute, I quitted my seat and walked on, though the thunder burst with a terrific crash over my head.

**Solution 2:** As the terrific crash of thunder burst over my head, and the darkness and storm increased by the minute, I quitted my seat and walked on.

SC practice prompts writers to manipulate syntax through rewriting kernel sentences in a manner similar to these examples (Ney, 1981; Strong, 1976; Weis, 1985). This practice is not unlike what skilled writers do as they work with their sentences. Skilled writers invest a great deal of time in thinking of different ways to say something. James Joyce, for example, would walk the streets while mentally rearranging the words of a single sentence until he was satisfied with the result.

Practice in combining sentences can benefit writers who, for example, rely mainly on simple sentences such as *My house is big. My house is brown.* to get their ideas across. Work with manipulating kernel sentences should help these writers explore different and more effective ways to state these same ideas—for example, *My house is big and brown* or *The big brown house is mine*—depending on what ideas they want to accentuate.

SC practice can help writers understand the choices available to them at the sentence level (Rhodes & Dudley-Marlin, 1996), including when and how to combine words and phrases. The "higher goal" of SC practice is really not just to create longer sentences, but to make "better" sentences—that is, sentences that more clearly convey writers' intended messages to readers. In fact, if there is a "trick" to SC, it is that SC practice helps students actually say more in fewer words (Strong, 1985).

## PART-TO-WHOLE LEARNING

Another powerful benefit of SC exercises is that writers can practice one small but important part of a bigger, more complex whole. Although some teachers may be reluctant to apply a "part-to-whole" learning process such as this, keep in mind that many acquired skills are practiced this way. As Elbow (1985) suggests, "Who could reasonably demand that nothing go on in writing courses except real writing? Exercises can help. I tried to play the viola and I find exercises helpful and even satisfying" (p. 233). But SC represents more than a typical worksheet-based, skill-drilling exercise. SC is both an exercise and "the real thing" (Elbow, 1985). A central part of the writing process is doing exactly what SC requires—namely, taking a set of already written sentences and transforming or manipulating them in order to improve them.

SC practice allows writers to systematically work through rhetorical problems they may encounter while creating and manipulating text during an actual writing experience. SC exercises begin by considering syntax only in sentences existing outside the context of a larger language picture; they then move to paragraph and whole-discourse analysis. Because the exercises are created in a sequential fashion from simple to more complex, students can incrementally improve their ability to handle producing, reading, judging, and modifying sentences (Gebhardt, 1985). The exercises allow students to wade slowly into the syntax "pool" from the shallow end, where they have a better chance of successfully learning to swim, instead of jumping into the deep end and floundering with syntactic manipulation.

There is no other writing activity that can accomplish this. As Moffett (1968) has suggested, "Only a comparison of sentence alternatives—in the context of what the author is trying to accomplish—will teach judgment" (p. 177). Accordingly, it's only through comparing various combinations of the same sentences that students can sense the slight changes to meaning various sentence combinations have and the effect those sentence changes may have on the overall meaning of the composition.

Before I present methods for teaching SC (Chapters 4–9), I first explain more fully the theoretical principles and the benefits of SC.

## THEORETICAL PRINCIPLES

The practice of SC is based on three theoretical principles (see Table 3.1 for a summary of these). The first principle is that student writers need instruction in formulating a clear understanding of what a written sentence actually is, the limits a simple sentence affords, and the syntactic options available to them for crafting a sentence (Neuleib & Fortune, 1985). In other words, SC practice can help writers learn and practice the language choices available to them (Nutter & Safran, 1983, 1984; see Stotski, 1975, for a review of research). It is true that professional writers may not typically write down strings of kernel sentences and then combine them as students will do while practicing SC: Skilled writers will draft a version, then adjust and revise that version (perhaps several times), before finally coming close to their vision or idea for the message. However, students can use SC practice to mimic this process of revision and adjustment by systematically trying out various sentence forms and exploring the options and syntactic alternatives available to them at the sentence level in their writing (Weis, 1985).

SC exercises, by presenting students with sets of simple sentences and requiring them to combine those sentences any way they wish as long as the product is grammatically correct, allow for the possibility of more than one "right" answer. This outcome—the awareness of the existence of acceptable alternatives—should be encouraged and can become itself a subject of instruction (Nutter & Safran, 1984). SC allows writers to adjust the placement of information in their sentences so as to transmit their message to their audience more effectively.

SC practice also encourages writers to tighten and clarify their thoughts by *decombining* lengthy sentences, or by rearranging, elaborating, or editing parts of sentences while also varying the sentence patterns appearing in paragraphs. In my own writing, as I am putting thoughts down, I routinely look back over what I have written and change the arrangements of words within my sentences, or I may combine sentences or add words to an existing sentence. These are routine acts for any mature writer, but for many young writers (including writers with disabilities), making effective syntactic decisions is very difficult, as they may not know the choices that are available to them. Such writers may need to hear and read many sentence constructions that would not initially come to mind. However, even hearing and

### TABLE 3.1. Theoretical Principles of Sentence Combining

1. Student writers need instruction in formulating a clear understanding of what a written sentence actually is, the limits a simple sentence affords, and the syntactic options available to them for crafting a sentence (Neuleib & Fortune, 1985).

2. The overall cognitive strain of writing is reduced once student writers become more comfortable and fluent with the process of sentence formation and re-formation (Graham, 1982).

3. Gains in syntactic fluency lead to high-quality writing (Strong, 1990).

reading are not enough for many writers with disabilities, who will also need to physically manipulate the syntax (Moffett, 1968, p. 168).

The second theoretical principle of SC instruction is that once student writers become more comfortable with and fluent in the process of sentence formation and re-formation, the overall cognitive strain of writing is reduced (Graham, 1982). The students can then free up cognitive space (i.e., "working memory") to attend to higher-level functions, including navigating the processes of writing, considering the audience's needs, and fulfilling the overall goals of an assignment. We humans use working memory to store and process information. Working memory has a limited capacity, however, so any activity that makes demands on working memory may interfere with another activity. In writing, if an activity such as handwriting, spelling, punctuation, or sentence construction occupies too great an amount of working memory, the writer has little "cognitive capital" left to use on the higher-level functions. This may have a direct impact on the writer's ability to produce ideas fluently. However, as writers manipulate syntactic structures through frequent SC practice, they may make their syntactic skills more automatic, and in doing so may release more working memory for higher-level tasks (Stotski, 1975). As Stotski (1975) puts it,

> The practice of playing mentally and operationally with syntactic structures leads to a kind of automatization of syntactic skills such that mental energy is freed . . . to concentrate on greater elaboration of intention and meaning. (1975, p. 55)

The third theoretical principle of SC instruction is that gains in syntactic fluency lead to high-quality writing (Strong, 1990). Research suggests that SC helps increase syntactic maturity or fluency in writers (Hunt, 1965). The reasoning behind this third principle is as follows: Because an important indicator of writing skill is syntactic fluency, if a writer makes gains in syntactic fluency, those gains may lead to high-quality writing (Strong, 1990). This makes obvious sense for two reasons. First, when teachers rate students' writing, they consider papers with a greater degree of syntactic maturity as higher in quality (Phillips, 1996). In addition, syntactic complexity elicits more favorable responses from competent readers (de Beaugrande, 1985).

## PRACTICAL BENEFITS OF SENTENCE COMBINING

Research suggests that SC practice may improve students' writing abilities in several significant and practical ways (see Table 3.2 for a summary of these benefits). First, by having student writers rework kernel sentences and later their own sentences, SC exercises help these writers "decenter," or think outside themselves to such a degree that they begin to understand how different syntactic options may affect readers (Strong, 1976; Neuleib & Fortune, 1985). Ideally, through this process of making judgments about their sentences and how the sentences will be received

**TABLE 3.2. Practical Benefits of Sentence Combining**

1. SC exercises help writers "decenter," or think outside themselves.
2. SC helps writers to make judgments about their sentences and to predict how the sentences will be received by an audience.
3. Discussing SC exercises may also help students become confident about punctuation (as well as capitalization and spelling).
4. SC practice may foster skill in revision.
5. SC practice may improve reading fluency and comprehension.

by an audience, they begin to consider how their writing sounds from the readers' perspective. These "decentering" skills are not only important on the sentence level, but are also critical to developing the overall flow and cohesiveness of the discourse.

Second, becoming aware of syntactic alternatives, through specific pattern drill and mindful manipulation of syntax, helps young writers to make judgments about their sentences and to predict how the sentences will be received by an audience. By elevating students' awareness that syntactic options exist in their writing, and by promoting their willingness to experiment with a wider range of those options, SC may increase the familiarity of syntactic patterns (de Beaugrande, 1985), and thereby improve students' linguistic performance by introducing them to sentence options (or transformations) not within their familiar spoken repertoires (Strong, 1985).

Greater familiarity with syntactic options may also boost students' confidence in their ability to manipulate sentence syntax, making them more willing to vary, experiment with, and try innovations in their writing. In other words, it may make them what O'Hare (1973) called "syntactical authorities," who are more able to overcome the monotonous style often found in the work of inexperienced or unskilled writers. With a rise in confidence or self-efficacy about trying new and different patterns, writers may be better able to achieve effective variety in their writing (de Beaugrande, 1985).

Applying alternatives to their writing may also help writers reduce the number of choppy or run-on sentences they typically produce (Gleason, 1962). Students may create such sentences while excluding better-formulated sentences, because they do not know the stylistic options available to them (Gleason, 1962). Gleason suggests that to be able to reduce choppy or run-on sentences, a writer must choose from a wide range of sentence patterns and, through the manipulation of those patterns, eventually create an arrangement that is more appealing to the reader.

Third, discussing SC exercises may also help students become confident about punctuation, as these exercises can illustrate how punctuation organizes sentence elements (Lindemann, 1995). The exercises can also prompt many discussions regarding the various types of punctuation that can be used in sentences. For example, when students combine sentences, a comma may be required, especially if a coordinating conjunction (*for, and, nor, but, or, yet, so*) is used as a connector. However, a comma should not be used if two sentences are combined without a connector (e.g., *The girl was pretty, the boy was handsome*). A comma can also be used after most introductory elements, especially long ones (e.g., *In the black car with the long slanted hood, the boy sat and hoped for time to pass quickly*), but can be left out if the introductory element is short (e.g., *In time the day became sunnier and happier for all*) or if the writer wishes to deemphasize the beginning of the sentence. SC provides a safe context for discussing not only punctuation, but capitalization and spelling as well. These discussions can naturally occur when a writer is trying new arrangements of words and ideas. Such discussions are likely to be much more effective than asking writers to complete worksheets on punctuation where no language is created or changed.

Fourth, SC practice may foster skill in revision. Revising has been called a process of transforming sentences (Elbow, 1985). SC can teach basic revision skills, such as expansion or reordering of ideas and tightening of language (Strong, 1985), and therefore may be extremely valuable in the revising stage of the writing process.

What we know about children's revising is that many adopt a least-effort strategy when revising sentences. That is, they will first make changes to the elements in the sentence that are easiest to alter, such as changing a word or adding punctuation, followed by slight elaborations (e.g., adding a descriptive word) and minor deletions (Hunt, 1983; Nodine et al., 1985). Their last choice, and the most cognitively challenging one, will be a partial or complete restructuring of their language. One reason for this may be that when revising, children tend to avoid tampering with "basic sentence plans," the ideas as initially set down in the form of sentences (Bereiter & Scardamalia, 1987; Hillocks, 1986). But even when children try to change these basic plans, often their revisions are not effective because the original versions, perceptually present on the page, have a direct claim on their conscious attention. Indeed, these versions can become such strong stimuli that they can literally block or inhibit the writer's ability to create new ways to state the same ideas (Bereiter & Scardamalia, 1987).

If the only alternatives available to a writer are those that come spontaneously to mind, revision has little chance of success, because unless the writer can deliberately bring alternatives to mind, the original text will "win" for lack of competition (Bereiter & Scardamalia, 1987). Even very skilled writers who can move beyond surface corrections and who display a readiness to take an audience into account in their syntactic choices may not recognize the relative value of various choices for their message. As a result, although they may appreciate the rhetorical impact of a particular choice, they settle too quickly and too adamantly on a particular choice without experimenting with other possibilities (Neuleib & Fortune, 1985).

Writers who make few revisions, or who settle on first choices without considering other syntactic options, need to gain mindful access to syntactic alternatives. These alternatives can help a writer transcend the original text on the page (Bereiter & Scardamalia, 1987). Bereiter and Scardamalia (1987), Hillocks (1986), and Hunt (1983) suggest that SC practice results in a hierarchically organized and systematic knowledge of syntactic structures that enables writers to thoughtfully consider alternatives in sentence structures (Hillocks, 1986). Furthermore, Hillocks (1987) suggests that SC is probably best used during the revision process, as it offers writers practice with alternative syntactic structures they can select for their own compositions.

Finally, there is some evidence to suggest that SC practice may improve reading fluency and comprehension (Graham & Hebert, 2010; Wilkinson & Patty, 1993). Although exactly why SC may have this impact on reading is not known, we can speculate that familiarity with the syntactic patterns experienced through SC practice may make the decoding of similar sentences more fluent when these are encountered in a reading selection. Furthermore, comprehension may be improved if the SC exercises are created from content the students are currently studying.

## SENTENCE COMBINING VERSUS "REAL" WRITING

SC is different from what might be considered "real" writing, in that students do not have to create what they want to say; the idea, or the "what," is already present in the content of the exercises. This is actually a strength rather than a limitation of SC practice, as all the students need to do is to figure out how to change and improve the basic sentences in the exercises. The provision of content may be a particularly useful component of SC practice for writers with disabilities, because they can practice expressing ideas without the pressure of creating ideas (Melvin, 1983). When student writers are provided with content, a key factor competing for working memory space is removed, allowing the writers to concentrate on comparing the actual text against their intentions and on modifying the developing text to match those intentions more closely (Gebhardt, 1985). The result is that students can learn to make effective adjustments to their developing text (Gebhardt, 1985). Also, because the exercises allow students to practice "style" with predetermined content, style is separated from meaning, allowing students to work on style in relative isolation from idea generation. In other words, the exercises permit students to distinguish what is said from how it is said (Melvin, 1983).

## RAISING METALINGUISTIC AWARENESS

Even when content is provided, transforming ideas is often not as simple as it may sound. Although many student writers will take to SC exercises very quickly without extensive instruction, others, especially writers with disabilities, may not understand what they need to do. Interestingly, even writers who understand how to perform the transformations without prompting may not be able to explain exactly how they chose to change the kernel sentences as they did. One reason for this may be that that SC exercises raise to a conscious level the metalinguistic skills needed to perform the transformations that are instinctual to many writers. In fact, Melvin

(1983) has suggested that much of a child's natural language learning may be an intuitive application of SC. According to Melvin, as children mature, they begin to combine several ideas into one expression or sentence organically. So in a sense, SC exercises may capitalize on what some children already know about language.

Even students who recognize that combining sentences is something they naturally carry out in their writing have probably not consciously considered just what they are doing when they rework their sentences. For these children, the exercises can help them become consciously aware of the subconscious process they are engaged in and may stimulate this seemingly naturally occurring cognitive growth.

In some ways, SC exercises represent puzzles to be solved through the application of logic and appear to be stimulating to writers on an intellectual level. Stotski (1975), for example, notes that SC may be especially effective at Piaget's logical-operational thought level (where reasoning processes are more closely linked to language), because intellectual growth at this stage is characterized by flexible and purposeful language manipulation.

## SENTENCE COMBINING
## VERSUS OTHER TYPES OF WRITING INSTRUCTION

SC is also different from other types of writing instruction, including sentence diagramming, grammar, and strategy instruction. Whereas sentence diagramming focuses on tearing a sentence apart into its basic grammatical elements, SC emphasizes the synthesis of ideas by focusing on putting sentences together (Strong, 1976). In other words, instead of learning to analyze or diagram sentences, writers learn to create them.

SC also provides a way to teach grammar and syntax without the grammatical terminology that can be so confusing to many students. When SC is practiced in a discovery-oriented environment, with students arriving at their own solutions to problems they are facing in their prose, writing may become more interesting and more rewarding (Smith, 1981), and students may learn from their errors rather than repeating them (Strong, 1985). In addition, because students use language naturally while making these transformations, rules need not be directly taught ahead of time, but are instead shown to the students within their writing; this helps them understand how the rules function within real language (Smith, 1981).

In the next chapter you will have an opportunity to practice combining sentences, so that you can experience the cognitive effort involved.

# PART II

TEACHING AND ASSESSMENT

CHAPTER 4

# The Cognitive Challenge
# of Combining Sentences

The best way to understand how SC works and what skills students need for engaging in SC practice sessions is to try several exercises and experience the cognitive challenges they present. Try to combine the two short sentences below into one sentence. Notice that in the second sentence the words *on my plate* are underlined. This underline is a clue indicating that these words must appear in the new combination.

- The noodle was soft.
- The noodle was <u>on my plate</u>.

**Solution:**

_____

_____

If you crafted a new sentence along the lines of *The soft noodle was on my plate*, you did well! You may also have thought of a different syntactic construction, such as *The noodle was on my plate and it was soft*; if that was your choice, it was a perfectly good one. Perhaps you created this syntactic gem: *On my plate was a soft noodle*. Nothing wrong with that one either.

Now, try the next example, which is slightly more challenging than the first. Once again, the underlined word *angry* must be included in your solution.

- The spaghetti was late.
- I was <u>angry</u>.

**Solution:**

_____

_____

Now these sentences offer several interesting choices. Perhaps you created the most obvious option: *The spaghetti was late and I was angry.* A grammatically correct solution, of course! Or you may have penned *I was angry because the spaghetti was late*, which certainly is a good choice, especially if you want to emphasize your anger. Using the connector *because* also creates a nice cause-and-effect relationship.

These first two exercises have been fairly simple, with only two sentences to combine. Now that you have the hang of combining, let's ratchet up the cognitive ante a bit. Try this exercise, and remember: Create a single sentence!

- The noodles were long.
- The noodles were skinny.
- The noddles fell on the floor.
- The noodles cracked into pieces.
- The dinner was ruined.

**Solution:**

_____

_____

What did you create with these sentences? Maybe you crafted something like *The long, skinny noodles fell on the floor, cracking into pieces and ruining the dinner.* Or perhaps you went with *The dinner was ruined when the long, skinny noodles fell on the floor and cracked into pieces.*

Perhaps as you were working through these sentences, you ran into syntactic difficulties that forced you to reevaluate your thinking. For example, what if you tried to start the sentence with *Ruining the dinner* and then tried to work in *the noodles cracked into pieces and fell on the floor.* Probably at that point you would have decided that you had missed *long* and *skinny,* so you placed these words in a position to tell more about the noodles, ending up with the solution *Ruining the dinner, the long, skinny noodles fell on the floor and cracked into pieces.* You may have decided at this point that the sentence did not flow exactly as you wanted, and so you shifted *ruining the dinner* to the end to create yet another option: *The long, skinny noodles fell on the floor and cracked into pieces, ruining the dinner.*

As you are now likely to understand, an exercise such as this third one is quite different from, and far more cognitively complex than, the first two. First, there are more sentences involved. Second, it includes no underlined words. The underlining indicates that certain information is important. When you read the first two sets of sentences, you automatically decided that the underlined words needed to be included in the new combination; all you had to do was decide how best to arrange the words. However, because the third example offers no such clues, you had to decide what information was important enough to retain and which could be eliminated from the new combination.

Although the third example is challenging, the difficulty of an exercise can be increased far more. For example, the following problem is lengthier and more complex. Try to combine the original sentences into five new sentences without losing any important information. My suggested solution follows.

### Left Out

Life is difficult.
This is true for left-handers.
They live in a world.
Everything is made for righties
 in this world.
Can openers are made for righties.
Scissors are made for righties.
School desks are made for righties.
Teachers often force lefties to write
 right-handed.
Coaches often force them to play
 right-handed.

But things may be changing.
Left-handers are organizing.
Left-handers are fighting for
 recognition.
They declared International
 Left-Handers' Day
This day was created in 1976.
It is on August 13.
Lefties win their "rights."
They won't be left out any more.

Based on Morenberg and Sommers (2003).

### Solution:

_____

_____

_____

_____

_____

_____

_____

_____

_____

_____

_____

_____

Here is my suggested solution:

### Left Out

Life is truly difficult for left-handers because they live in a world where everything, including can openers, scissors, and school desks, is made for righties. Lefties are even forced by teachers to write right-handed, and coaches often force them to play right-handed. But things are changing for lefties, because they are organizing and fighting for recognition. In fact, in 1976, lefties declared August 13 International Left-Handers' Day. When lefties win their "rights," they won't be left out any more.

This exercise, presented without underlined clues, offers a complex syntactic puzzle. However, the cognitive operations involved in deciding on an effective recombination mimic the same steps a writer might follow in writing and rewriting text.

Think about the steps you took while creating your solution. What "mental gymnastics" did you engage in? Reflecting on your own experiences with SC will help you teach these skills to your students.

In the next chapter I discuss two general types of SC exercises: "cued" and "open."

CHAPTER 5

# Types of Sentence-Combining Exercises

Before introducing SC to your students, you will need to create exercises. Unfortunately, there are no nationally recognized SC curricula available that work for each grade level; fortunately, however, SC exercises are very easy to create.

In general, SC exercises move from very simple kernel problems that offer only a limited number of possible solutions to paragraph and whole-discourse problems that can be solved in a wide variety of ways. Exercises can be created to teach many aspects of writing, including grammatical elements, sentence and syntactic arrangements, intersentential coherence and paragraph construction, punctuation, capitalization, coherence, tone, emphasis, and style.

There are two basic types of SC exercises: "cued" or "open." You have tried both types of exercises in Chapter 4. Either type provides a contrived context in which writers can experiment with a variety of sentence output functions (Crowhurst & Piche, 1979; Strong, 1986) and can learn—by combining, decombining, and recombining—how to say more in fewer words (Gebhardt, 1985; Miller & Ney, 1968; Stotski, 1975).

## CUED EXERCISES

The more basic exercises, and the ones that should be used initially when you are introducing SC, are "cued" or "signaled." Cued exercises offer specific clues to prompt students to combine the kernels in a certain way. Two types of clues can be used: underlined clues and key words placed within parentheses.

## Underlined Clues

An exercise featuring an underlined clue will look similar to this example:

The water was cold.
The water was refreshing.

Notice that the two sentences are as similar as possible, except for the words to be combined. Try to create a new sentence from these kernels:

_____

There are many possible solutions for these kernels that can be formed without adding words or changing any words. Consider these examples:

The water was cold and refreshing.
The water was refreshing and cold.
The cold water was refreshing.
The refreshing water was cold.

Perhaps one of my solutions was the same as yours.

When you are introducing a problem with an underlined clue, explain to the students that the underlined word in the second sentence is an important piece of information that needs to be included in the new sentence combination. Students need to be aware that this information cannot be left out of the new combination. Also explain that there is information in the second sentence (in the exercise above, *the water was*) that is redundant and that does not need to be written in the new combination. You may also want to show a combination such as this:

Was the water cold and refreshing?

This particular combination is a nice example of how to arrange sentence elements in such a way to change a statement into a question.

## Key Words Placed within Parentheses

The second method to cue a particular combination is to include a key word enclosed in parentheses at the end of the sentence to be combined, as in this example:

The girl fell over the log.
She lost her balance. (because)

Try to create a new sentence from these kernels:

_____

Several combinations of these kernels are possible:

> Because she lost her balance, the girl fell over the log.
> The girl fell over the log because she lost her balance.
> Because she fell over the log, the girl lost her balance.

Notice that this exercise would also be handy to explain the use (or nonuse) of a comma to separate and organize sentence elements.

You can also combine underlined and parenthetical cues in exercises, as in this example:

> Manny Ramirez is a baseball player.
> Manny first played for the Cleveland Indians. (who)

Try to create a new sentence from these kernels:

_____

Here is one possible combination for these kernels:

> Manny Ramirez is a baseball player who first played for the Cleveland Indians.

Using both types of clues is helpful for students who may not be able to decide which information in the second kernel is important enough to keep in the new combination.

Cued exercises can also include a clue word that leads to a very specific combination. In this example, the subordinate conjunction *who* is used to create complex sentences with a dependent clause:

> The announcer introduced the batter.
> The batter had hit a home run in the first inning. (who)

Try to create a new sentence from these kernels:

_____

Perhaps you created a sentence such as this:

> The announcer introduced the batter who had hit a home run in the first inning.

Notice that in this example there really is only one combination that can be created, because the cue is so specific. Cued SC exercises with specific syntactic directions, such as this last example, can give students opportunities for mindful, systematic practice with specific syntactic options. They are thus valuable for acquainting students with particular sentence structures. Think of these exercises as a means of helping students think about language in a very precise way, while also providing enough practice in using a particular combination to make them comfortable applying it in their writing.

Table 5.1 provides three guidelines suggested by Strong (1986) to help you create effective cued exercises.

Let's try a few additional cued exercises before moving on. Try to combine these four kernel sentence clusters (possible solutions are provided below the clusters).

1.  The rain fell.
    The rain was <u>cold</u>.
    Combination:

    _____

2.  The winds blew.
    The winds were <u>strong</u>.
    Combination:

    _____

3.  I will stay inside.
    It is cold and windy outside. (because)
    Combination:

    _____

### TABLE 5.1. Guidelines for Creating Effective Cued Exercises

1.  Set up the exercises so that the base clause comes first, followed by one or more modifying sentences. For example:

    Base sentence:          The dog ran.

    Modifying sentence:  The dog was wet.

    Combination:            The wet dog ran.

2.  Place connecting words in parentheses following the sentence in which they appear. For example:

    I like to write.

    I am very smart. (because)

    Combination: I like to write because I am very smart.

3.  Underline words or phrases that need to be embedded into the base sentence. For example:

    I like to write sentences.

    The sentences are <u>interesting</u>.

    Combination: I like to write interesting sentences.

*Note.* Based on Strong (1986).

4. I like to read.
 I can't take a walk outside. (when)
 Combination:

_____

### Possible Solutions:

1. The cold rain fell.
2. The strong winds blew.
3. I will stay inside because it is cold and windy outside.
4. I like to read when I can't take a walk outside.

After students are comfortable with combining two kernels with a cue, add more sentences to increase the complexity of the exercise. For example:

The ball sailed over the fence.
The team laughed.
The team cheered.

Try to create a new sentence from these kernels:

_____

Perhaps you created a sentence such as this:

The ball sailed over the fence as the team laughed and cheered.

Exercises that include multiple kernels can be much more difficult for students. Yet they are a necessary step up the ladder of syntactic complexity. These exercises can offer multiple solutions and can stimulate lively discussions about the various alternatives possible. Take the following exercise, for example:

### The Cobra

The snake was lying in the grass.
The snake was a cobra.

A mouse ran by.
The mouse was tiny.
It ran quickly.
It ran all of a sudden.

The cobra struck.
It struck instantly.
The cobra was deadly.

The sentences in "The Cobra" can be combined in many different ways. Here is just one example:

> The cobra snake was lying in the grass. All of a sudden a tiny mouse quickly ran by. The deadly cobra struck instantly.

When exercises contain many sentences to combine, you can require students to create a solution that contains a certain number of sentences. Although such a restriction will increase the difficulty of the exercise, it will eliminate the possibility that the students will make only one or two combinations in their solutions.

Although cued or signaled exercises such as "The Cobra"—initially presented as pairs of kernels, and later as sets of three or more sentences—are the best ways to introduce the concept of SC, such exercises should not be relied on exclusively, as they have limitations. First, because these problems are presented in isolation, they lack relationships to or context within a larger whole. Often context is needed to weigh the qualitative value of one particular combination over another. In addition, students can become overly captivated with certain constructions practiced during the exercises and may use them arbitrarily within a composition, without any consideration for the suitability of these constructions in that particular context. In other words, the exercises offer no opportunity for the students to ask these important questions in rhetoric: Which phrasing is most effective in this context? Which is most conducive to persuading the audience of the truth of my point? (Neman, 1995). Finally, as Neman (1995) suggests, cued problems have cued solutions; once new concepts are mastered, these exercises can become as sterile and unprofitable as more traditional grammar exercises if they are overused, or used exclusively.

## OPEN EXERCISES

The second, and more complex, type of SC exercise for students is the "open" exercise, where a set of kernels must be combined without a cue word. In these exercises, many sentence combinations are possible. Because no clues are provided, students must also decide what important material in the second sentence to include within the first when the two are combined. Consider this example:

> The girl lifted the glass.
> The glass was white.

Initially you may need to explain to the students that the word *white* in the second sentence offers new information and should be included in the new combination. By including *white* in the new combination and by eliminating unnecessary information, you can make the following combinations:

> The girl lifted the white glass.
> The white glass was lifted by the girl.

The girl lifted the glass that was white.
White was the glass that the girl lifted.
The glass lifted by the girl was white.

Once students are comfortable with combining two kernel sentences without clues, introduce exercises that require combining sequences of three or more kernel sentences without clues. For example:

The book fell.
The book was large.
The book was heavy.
It fell from the shelf.
It didn't hit anyone.

This group of sentences may elicit many interesting combinations. Try to create three different combinations in the blanks provided, and then read my suggestions below the blanks.

1. _____

_____

2. _____

_____

3. _____

_____

Here are my solutions:

The large, heavy book fell from the shelf hitting no one.
Falling from the shelf, the large, heavy book hit no one.
Falling from the shelf, the large, heavy book did not hit anyone.
The book that fell from the shelf was large and heavy, but it did not hit anyone.
Though large and heavy, the book that fell from the shelf did not hit anyone.

Now here is a second example:

The wind blew.
The wind was strong.
It blew through the window.
The window was open.
It knocked the glass over.

Again, try to create three different combinations, and then read my suggestions below the blanks.

1. _____

_____

2. _____

_____

3. _____

_____

Here are my solutions:

The strong wind blew through the open window, knocking over the glass.
The glass was knocked over by the strong wind that blew through the open window.
Blowing through the open window, the strong wind knocked over the glass.

## CHECKING ACCURACY

Sometimes with open exercises that include many kernel sentences, students may exclude key bits of information when creating a new combination. One way to ensure that the students include the important information in the new combination is to have students circle all of the important information in the kernels and then number each circle. Next, tell them to circle all of the important information in the combined sentences. Then number each of the circles in the combined sentence to correspond with the numbering in the kernels. Try to use this coding method to check the accuracy of these solutions, and then use the example that follows the solutions to check your work.

**Problem:**  The book fell.

The book was large.

It fell from the shelf.

**Solutions:**  1.  The book fell from the shelf.

2.  The large book fell from the shelf.

The book (fell.)[1]

The book was (large)[2]

It fell (from the shelf)[3]

**Solutions:**  1.  The book (fell)[1] (from the shelf)[3]

2.  The (large)[2] book (fell)[1] (from the shelf)[3]

Clearly, solution 1 is missing information about the book that needs to be included. Solution 2 has incorporated all of the important information. After this type of self-checking, the students should be prompted to include any missing information. This method allows students to check the accuracy of their own solutions and is a great way to promote careful reading. Ensuring accuracy in the combinations is a parallel skill to other academic tasks (e.g., summarizing a reading selection or taking notes), where students must reread their work to ensure that important information has been retained.

## WHOLE-DISCOURSE EXERCISES

Eventually, when your students are comfortable with combining multiple kernel sentences with and without clues, you will need to move from sentence-level to paragraph-level practice. Problems of this length are referred to as "whole-discourse exercises."

A whole-discourse exercise presents a set of kernel sentences that are sequenced to allow the writer to create a paragraph or a short story about a subject. The example that follows is a story-length open SC exercise based loosely on the old fable about the boy who cried wolf.

A boy kept a flock of sheep.
The boy was a shepherd.
He kept the sheep at a distance from
   the village.

He thought he would play a trick.
The trick was on the village people.
The trick was for fun.

He ran to the town.
He yelled about a wolf.
The wolf was eating his sheep.
The villagers ran to the meadow.
They ran quickly.
They ran to help the boy.

The boy laughed.
He laughed at the villagers.

The villagers were angry.
They were angry with the boy.

The boy tried the trick again.
He tried it the next day.
The trick was on the villagers.

The villagers ran to the meadow.
They ran quickly.
They ran to help the boy.

The boy laughed again.
He laughed at the villagers.

The villagers were really angry.
They were angry with the boy.
The wolf came.
It was the next day.
It came to eat the sheep.

The boy shouted.
The shout was for help.
The shout was to the villagers.

The villagers did not come.
They did not believe the boy.
The boy had played tricks on them.

The boy could not save the sheep.
The sheep had to save themselves.
The sheep had to run away.

Try to combine these sentences in the blanks below, and then check beneath the blanks for one potential solution to this problem.

_____

_____

_____

_____

_____

_____

_____

_____

_____

_____

_____

_____

_____

_____

_____

_____

_____

_____

_____

| A boy kept a flock of sheep. The boy was a shepherd. He kept the sheep at a distance from the village. | A shepherd boy kept a flock of sheep at a distance from the village. |

| | |
|---|---|
| He thought he would play a trick.<br>The trick was on the village people.<br>The trick was for fun. | He thought he would play a trick on the village people for fun. |
| He ran to the town.<br>He yelled about a wolf.<br>The wolf was eating his sheep.<br>The villagers ran to the meadow.<br>They ran quickly.<br>They ran to help the boy. | He ran to the town while yelling that a wolf was eating his sheep. The villagers quickly ran to the meadow to help the boy. |
| The boy laughed.<br>He laughed at the villagers. | The boy laughed at the villagers. |
| The villagers were angry.<br>They were angry with the boy. | The villagers were angry with the boy. |
| The boy tried the trick again.<br>He tried it the next day.<br>The trick was on the villagers. | The boy tried the trick on the villagers again the next day. |
| The villagers ran to the meadow.<br>They ran quickly.<br>They ran to help the boy. | The villagers quickly ran to the meadow to help the boy. |
| The boy laughed again.<br>He laughed at the villagers. | The boy laughed again at the villagers. |
| The villagers were really angry.<br>They were angry with the boy.<br>The wolf came.<br>It was the next day.<br>It came to eat the sheep. | The villagers were really angry with the boy. The next day a wolf came to eat the sheep. |
| The boy shouted.<br>The shout was for help.<br>The shout was to the villagers. | The boy shouted to the villagers for help. |
| The villagers did not come.<br>They did not believe the boy.<br>The boy had played tricks on them. | The villagers did not believe the boy and did not come because the boy had played tricks on them. |
| The boy could not save the sheep.<br>The sheep had to save themselves.<br>The sheep had to run away. | The sheep saved themselves by running away because the boy could not save them. |

Clearly, there is a lot to consider in combining so many sentences (including which sentences to combine, which words to leave out, what words can be changed, etc.). Because of the number of decisions to be made, the cognitive effort is increased dramatically when students combine multiple kernel sentences—to the point where you may need to work through the first few exercises cluster by cluster, discussing examples of various combinations until the last clusters are combined.

Although whole-discourse exercises are cognitively more challenging, they avoid many of the limitations of cued exercises because they offer a far more naturalistic writing environment; that is, they are much more like "real" writing. Open exercises of this length offer a chance to combine sentences within the context of a paragraph and story so that "intersentential coherence," or the degree to which sentences fit together and support each other, can be considered. This is the next logical skill after a writer becomes fluent with creating individual sentences.

To help students bridge the syntactic gap between sentences and paragraphs, instruction must help shift attention from the sentence to the paragraph level. If a text is cohesive on the sentence level, all of the sentences logically fit together, and support one another, and the overall discourse has a coherent flow that makes sense to a reader. To create cohesive sentences, a writer often has to reformulate parts of the text. When engaged in this process, the writer may discover that a change in one sentence frequently calls for a change in the next. This process should lead the writer to verify the clarity (in terms of substance and expression) of the message for the intended reader.

Development of this critical facility is best practiced with extended or whole-discourse exercises that include an extensive amount of discussion. As Strong (1985) suggests, paragraph and later whole-discourse SC exercises, because of their built-in logic and organization, help increase students' awareness of mental "moves" in writing—includng general-to-specific paragraphing, comparison/contrast, use of transitions, and relating old and new information.

Students can practice creating a unified whole by leading one sentence into another and by logically arranging the sentences into a paragraph so that they support one another. These exercises also offer the chance for students to explore the effects of various syntactic decisions on the overall style of the piece and on the coherence, tone, and emphasis of ideas, as well as the effects a change in rhythm of one sentence may have on others.

While students are completing the multiple-sentence exercises, directly encourage them toward greater variety: Suggest that the more sentence structures they use comfortably in their writing, the more interesting the writing will become to their readers. Your students are likely to be impressed by the number of different combinations that these few kernels produce, and they will enjoy comparing the results of their efforts (Neman, 1995).

Whole-discourse exercises can be expanded by having students revise the paragraph after they initially combine the sentences. For example, many of the sentences in the new paragraph may start with *the*. You can challenge students to vary the beginnings of the sentences as a fun revising exercise. You can also have them try to reduce the number of sentences in the paragraph without losing any important information. The revised final solutions that the students create will make an interesting display for a bulletin board in your classroom.

Whole-discourse exercises can also be used to target specific skills. For example, paragraphs written mostly with short, choppy sentences are ideal for modeling compound sentences, whereas paragraphs with run-ons and sentence fragments are perfect for helping students understand the purpose of punctuation marks in delineating sentence boundaries. Paragraphs that have many sentences beginning with *then* are good for modeling subordinate clauses for time relationships. Descriptive paragraphs can have additional adjective clauses or appositives added for more sophisticated-sounding sentences.

Even though open exercises are very valuable, they present several potential perils (Neman, 1995). First, students may just serially connect sentences without performing a single transformation, creating a rambling wreck of a composition. Second, there is an increased likelihood of grammatical errors somewhere in the new combinations. But despite these potential perils, open exercises offer a challenging way for students to experiment with language and explore the effects of choices on the intended message. That is, do the choices help them to say something in a better way?

## RAMPING UP CUED AND OPEN EXERCISES

The systematic nature of SC allows exercises to begin very simply and become more sophisticated as students' skills and familiarity with SC increase. A logical sequence of simple to more complex is as follows:

1. Begin with two kernel sentences with clues. For example:

   Tony is a man.
   He is <u>happy</u>.

   Or

   Tony is happy.
   He has lots of money. (because)

2. Progress to three or more kernel sentences with clues. For example:

   The Civil War was fought between two groups of states.
   The war was a <u>long and bloody struggle</u>.
   The states were the <u>Northern and Southern</u>.

3. Progress to three or more kernel sentences with clues that represent one paragraph. For example:

> The boat was in the water.
> The water was <u>cold</u>.
> The water was <u>salty</u>.

> A storm came.
> It came <u>suddenly</u>.
> The storm was <u>fierce</u>.

> The boat began to sink.
> It sank <u>slowly</u>.

> The men jumped.
> They were <u>frightened</u>.
> They <u>landed in the water</u>.
> The water was <u>swirling</u>.

4. Progress to two or more multiple-kernel-sentence clusters with clues that represent two paragraphs.
5. Progress to two or more multiple-kernel-sentence clusters with clues that represent three or more paragraphs.
6. Follow the sequence above (1–5) without clues.
7. Then follow this same sequence (1–5) with some combinations cued and some without clues, eventually reaching an exercise such as the following:

> 1. He paid the bills.
>    He left the restaurant.
>    He started walking through the streets. (and)
>    His melancholy growing more and more beautiful.

> 2. He had spent years of life.
>    He had spent them with Tereza.
>    The years were seven.
>    He now realized something.
>    He realized those years were more attractive. (that)
>    They were more attractive in retrospect.
>    They were <u>more attractive</u> than when he was living them.

> From *The Unbearable Lightness of Being* by Milan Kundera (1984).

## TRANSFER TO CONNECTED WRITING

For both cued and open exercises, it is critical that the students transfer the knowledge gained through practice to their writing, or the exercises will lose much of their value. This transfer involves making concrete connections between skill-building SC exercises and connected writing. The students must understand how SC improves their writing. Several methods can help students to make this transfer:

1. Continually prompt and encourage students to use the learned constructions appropriately in their writing.
2. Use the students' own writing, or the material they are reading, to create exercises. Specifying contexts for writing, including particular situations, purposes, and audiences, makes the exercises more functional and interesting; in turn, this makes the skills more readily available when students create their own compositions.
3. Create parallel writing tasks for the application of target skills to help students make connections. To do this, you can direct students to include the constructions they are practicing in their writing. A second type of parallel writing task is to ask students to decombine sentences in a piece they are currently writing—that is, to make kernel sentences out of the sentences in a composition. The students can then recombine the kernels and compare the results to the original sentences.
4. The exercises themselves can help promote transfer if they are spontaneous, naturally occurring samples that students might actually write, or preferably ones that they did write (de Beaugrande, 1985).

## CONTENT SOURCES FOR EXERCISES

With these considerations in mind, creating the exercises becomes your next concern. Exercises can be created from a wide variety of sources, including the students' own writing, literature series you are using in your classroom, authentic grade-level literature or trade books, content-area texts, magazines, or any other print source available to you (including online sources). Many of these sources offer the added benefit of providing content-related information that may either reinforce or introduce a concept you are teaching.

For example, here are two exercises created from sections of social studies textbooks. The first is from an elementary text; the other is from a high school text.

### Elementary Social Studies Content

Washington was famous.
He was our first president. (because)

Washington was a president.
Lincoln was a president. (and)

---

They were famous.
They helped many people. (because)

---

Lincoln has a big monument.
Washington's monument is taller. (but)

---

### High School Social Studies Content

Britain waged a different kind of war.
Germany waged a different kind of war.

They waged this war by flooding the United States with propaganda.
The propaganda was sent in the mail.
Most of what the U.S. heard about the war was through the mail. (because)

---

---

---

Classroom activities or school happenings can also be sources for exercises. These sources may be particularly motivating for students to write about, as their personal knowledge of and interest in them can support their learning. Personal stories and anecdotes from the students' own lives are also great sources for exercises. Knowledge the students share about themselves can be fun to write about and can help build community and personal involvement in your classroom of writers.

As mentioned earlier, the best source for exercises is the students' own writing. Using their writing as the source for exercises can engage students at their level of need and understanding, while providing direct resolutions for problems associated with a current piece of writing. Exercises created from their own prose help students to work and rework their own ideas, and thereby to practice controlling and manipulating the syntactic options available to them within their actual writing (Strong, 1986).

Any of these sources can be turned into exercises by simply reducing or decombining a passage into kernel sentences that match the combining technique you want your students to practice. Again, decombining involves reducing a passage back to kernel sentences by breaking apart long sentences into shorter sentences that can be easily recombined. In other words, it involves creating an SC problem from a short passage of text. When you are decombining text, your goal is to create kernels that are straightforward and easily recombined, with logical cues for recombining that allow the recombination to follow the original passage. Also, you need to make decombined clusters for each sentence in the original.

Here is an example of a passage from the story "Gloria Who Might Be My Best Friend" by Ann Cameron (1981):

> We ran through the back yard with the kite, passed the garden and the fig tree, and went into the open field beyond our yard.
> The kite started to rise. The tail jerked heavily like a long white snake. In a minute the kite passed the roof of my house and was climbing toward the sun.

And here is the same passage decombined into an SC exercise:

*First Sentence*

> We ran through the back yard with the kite, passed the garden and the fig tree, and went into the open field beyond our yard.

1. We ran through the back yard.
   We ran with the kite.
   We passed the garden.
   We passed the fig tree.
   We went into the field.
   The field was open.
   The field was beyond our yard.

*Second and Third Sentences*

> The kite started to rise. The tail jerked heavily like a long white snake.

2. The kite started.
   It started to rise
3. The tail jerked.
   It jerked heavily.
   It jerked like a long white snake.

*Fourth Sentence*

> In a minute the kite passed the roof of my house and was climbing toward the sun.

4. The kite passed.
   It passed in a minute.
   It passed the roof of my house.
   It was climbing toward the sun.

Here is an example from geography content:

## High School Geography

### LOCATION

Every point on Earth has a specific location that is determined by an imaginary grid of lines denoting latitude and longitude. Parallels of latitude measure distances north and south of the line called the Equator. Meridians of longitude measure distances east and west of the line called the Prime Meridian.

And here is the same passage decombined:

Every point on Earth has a specific location.
That location is determined by an imaginary grid of lines.
The lines denote latitude.
The lines denote longitude.
Parallels of latitude measure distances north and south of a line.
The line is called the Equator.
Meridians of longitude measure distances east and west of a line.
The line is called the Prime Meridian.

Decombining may seem like a difficult task, but it will become much easier with practice. Several segments of text are provided below, to help you gain confidence with your decombining ability.

The first passage is taken from the book *If You Lived in Colonial Times* by Ann McGovern (1964). Try to decombine the passage sentence by sentence, and then compare your solution to the exemplars provided.

Sometimes the schoolmaster had more food than he could eat. That happened once to a schoolmaster in the town of Salem. The schoolmaster had too much corn. So he made one of the boys stand near an open window. When the boy saw someone walking by, he tried to trade the extra corn for something the schoolmaster could use.

**Sentence 1:** Sometimes the schoolmaster had more food than he could eat.

_____

_____

**Sentence 1 solution:**
The schoolmaster had food.
He had food sometimes.
He had more food than he could eat.

**Sentence 2:** That happened once to a schoolmaster in the town of Salem.

_____

_____

**Sentence 2 solution:**
> That happened once.
> It happened to a schoolmaster.
> It was in the town of Salem.

**Sentence 3:** The schoolmaster had too much corn.

_____

_____

**Sentence 3 solution:**
> The schoolmaster had corn.
> He had too much.

**Sentence 4:** So he made one of the boys stand near an open window.

_____

_____

**Sentence 4 solution:**
> He made one of the boys stand. (so)
> The boy stood near a window.
> The window was open.

**Sentence 5:** When the boy saw someone walking by, he tried to trade the extra corn for something the schoolmaster could use.

_____

_____

**Sentence 5 solution:**
> The boy saw someone. (when)
> He saw someone walking by.
> He tried to trade the corn.
> The corn was extra.
> He tried to trade for something the schoolmaster could use.

Now try to create an exercise from the following segment. My suggested solution is provided below, after the blanks.

British troops found fighting in America very challenging, because they were trained to fight wars in Europe. The European armies stood shoulder to shoulder, and the soldiers fired shots at each other until one side broke and ran. In America, the colonial soldiers did not fight this way. They would hide behind trees and fire at the British troops.

_____

_____

_____

_____

_____

_____

_____

_____

_____

Compare your exercise with my suggestion:

British troops found fighting in America very challenging.
They were trained to fight wars in Europe. (because)

The European armies stood shoulder to shoulder.
Soldiers fired shots at each other.
They fired until one side broke and ran.

The colonial soldiers did not fight this way.
The colonial soldiers were in America.

They would hide behind trees.
They would fire at the British troops.

Here is an additional example that you can try. This one is from Mary Shelley's (1818/2003) *Frankenstein*. Again, my suggested solution is provided below, after the blanks.

Remember, I am not recording the vision of a madman. The sun does not more certainly shine in the heavens than that which I now affirm is true. Some miracle might have produced it, yet the stages of the discovery were distinct and probable. After days and nights of incredible labor and fatigue, I succeeded in discovering the cause of generation and life; nay, more, I became myself capable of bestowing animation upon lifeless matter.

_____

_____

_____

_____

_____

_____

_____

_____

_____

Now check your solution against my version:

1.  I am not recording a vision.
    The vision is of a <u>madman</u>.
    Remember that.

2.  The sun does not more certainly shine.
    It shines in the <u>heavens</u>.
    I now affirm it is true. (than that which)

3.  Some miracle produced it.
    The stages of the discovery were distinct. (yet)
    The stages of the discovery were probable.

4.  I succeeded in discovering the cause of generation.
    I discovered the cause of <u>life</u>.
    The success was after days of incredible labor and fatigue.
    The success was after <u>nights</u> of incredible labor and fatigue.

5.  Nay, more, I became capable of bestowing animation.
    The bestowing was upon lifeless matter. (myself)

Here is one final example of a passage for you to decombine. The source is a newspaper story about weather, and, as you can see, a great deal of information is presented in the two sentences.

## Wind, Tornadoes, Storms to Settle Down

Weather will be calming down today after a wild two-day storm that pummeled the Midwest and Southeast. Punishing wind, tornadoes, and snow left tens of thousands without electricity, dozens injured, extensive property damage, and travel havoc.

## Decombined Sentence 1

Weather will be calming down.
It will be calming today.
It will be calming after a storm.
The storm was wild.
The storm lasted two days.
The storm pummeled the Midwest.
The storm pummeled the Southeast.

## Decombined Sentence 2

There was wind.
The wind was punishing.
There were tornadoes.
There was snow.
People were without electricity.
There were tens of thousands without electricity.
Dozens were injured.
There was extensive property damage.
There was travel havoc.

Before beginning to teach SC, you may want to teach the basics of a sentence to your class. In the next chapter I provide scripted lessons to help with your instruction.

CHAPTER 6

# Teaching Sentences

Since SC is a sentence-level intervention, students should have a certain level of knowledge about sentences, and should be able to create them, before beginning to learn how to combine them. This level of knowledge doesn't need to be extensive, but it's wise to ensure that students understand what a sentence is and realize that words/ideas can be added to sentences. This initial practice will help with later SC discussions. Depending on the grade level and skill levels involved, this information may be a review, or it may be completely new. Either way, the point is to provide a foundational level of knowledge for your students.

The following teaching scripts follow a "learn–see–do" structure while introducing the elements of a basic sentence. The script can be modified to fit various abilities or ages by creating new sentences matching the students' reading levels. In addition, you may have to provide more sample sentences for students who may require more extensive practice.

## SENTENCE BASICS 1

**Goal:** In this lesson students will define a sentence and will provide samples of sentences.

1. Start by saying, "Can anyone tell me what a 'sentence' is?" Elicit responses from students.
2. Then say, "Here is a good definition of a sentence: a word or a group of words telling one or more than one complete thoughts that begins with a capital letter, ends with some kind of punctuation, and makes sense."
3. "It's easier to understand what a sentence is when we look at examples of sentences and examples of word groups that are not sentences."

4. "Here are three different sentences [have the three sentences displayed so that students can read them along with you]. Follow along as I read them to you."

> The sky was gray.
> The batter hit the ball.
> I left my heart in San Francisco.

5. "Each of these groups of words meets our definition of a sentence."

6. "Here are three groups of words that are not sentences [display the next three so that students can read them along with you]. Follow along as I read them to you."

> The sky was
> The batter
> I left my

7. Ask, "Why are these groups of words not sentences?" Wait for responses. Make sure that the students understand that the groups of words are not sentences because they do not tell a complete thought, do not make sense, and do not include end punctuation.

8. "These groups of words are called 'sentence fragments' because they are only part of a sentence. In most cases you should not use sentence fragments in your writing."

9. "Let's try to add words to these fragments to make them sentences." Write down ideas for each sentence from several students. Read each complete sentence, comparing each to the definition.

10. "These sentences all tell us a complete thought; they begin with a capital letter; they end with some kind of punctuation; and they make sense."

11. "During the next lesson we will practice writing very short sentences, and we will learn what the basic parts of a sentence are called."

## SENTENCE BASICS 2

**Goal:** In this lesson the students will create simple noun–verb sentences.

1. Begin by asking, "Can anyone think of a very short sentence?" Write several examples of short sentences on an overhead projector, SMART Board, or blackboard. Students might suggest sentences similar to these:

> The room is hot.
> The dog jumped into the bowl.
> I ran home.

2. "Good. These are all sentences because they are groups of words telling one or more than one complete thought; they begin with a capital letter; they end with some kind of punctuation; and they make sense."

3. "Now let's see if you can make sentences that are even shorter. Can anyone make a sentence from just two words?" Write several examples of short sentences on the overhead projector, SMART Board, or blackboard. Students might provide examples such as these:

> Heat rises.
> Dogs bark.
> Boats float.
> Ice melts.

4. "Are these sentences? Check our definition, please."

5. "These are very short sentences. These are called 'simple sentences,' and they are a good starting point to learn how to make sentences."

6. "These simple sentences contain two important parts: a 'noun' and a 'verb.' A noun can be a person, place, object, or idea. A verb tells something about the noun. Let's find the noun and verb in the sentences we just wrote." Ask for volunteers to state which word is the noun and which is the verb in each of the sentences.

7. "During the next lesson we will take these short sentences and make them longer."

## SENTENCE BASICS 3

**Goal:** In this lesson the students will expand short sentences by adding additional details.

1. Begin by saying, "Let's look at the sentences we wrote in the last lesson." Have several sentences from the prior lesson written out so that the class can read them.

2. "Simple sentences like these with just a noun and a verb are easy to make, but what if we had an entire story that only contained simple sentences? Here is a story that contains only very short, simple sentences." Show the story while reading it aloud.

### A Fun Day

Sun rose. Birds sang. Dogs barked. Boy walked. Balloon burst.
Girl laughed. Boy cried.

3. "Did you enjoy that story? Why or why not?" Elicit students' responses.

4. "A story filled with short sentences is actually very challenging to write and can get boring to read. It's better to use a variety of sentences in a story, including some that are longer than these. Readers will have an easier time reading your writing and will enjoy what you wrote more if you include a variety of sentences in your writing."

5. "Let's try to add ideas to these short sentences to make them more interesting to a reader."

6. "Let me show you an example. This sentence—*Dogs barked*—does not tell us a whole lot. A reader would want to know more information. For example, what kind of dogs were they? Why were they barking? What did their bark sound like?"

7. "I am going to add several ideas to this sentence that will help my reader understand more about these barking dogs."

8. "First I am going to tell more about the dogs by adding the word *big*." Add this word to the sentence and read aloud.

9. "Next I will tell something about the dogs' bark. The bark was very loud, so I will add *loudly* to the sentence." Add this word to the sentence and read aloud.

10. "Now our sentence is more interesting, but we can still add more information. Let's see, maybe we can tell what the dogs were barking at. I think they were barking at a cat, so I will add that to the sentence." Add a phrase to the sentence and read aloud: "*The big dogs barked loudly at the cat.*"

11. "We can add even more to this sentence by connecting another sentence with this one. For example, we could add the sentence *The cat was not scared*. If I add this new sentence to the old sentence, I will have to add a word to connect the two sentences together. I will use the connector *but*." Add sentence and connector, and read aloud: "*The big dogs barked loudly at the cat, but the cat was not scared.*"

12. "We have created quite a long sentence that tells the reader a lot of information about the dogs. Let's add information to the other short sentences that we wrote during the last lesson, to make them longer and more interesting also." At this point you can have students work together to add details to the short sentences, or you can have each student work independently. Either way, have several students share their new sentences with the class.

13. "During the next lesson we will start practicing a writing activity called 'sentence combining' that will help us learn different ways to make short, simple sentences longer and more interesting."

In the next chapter I provide specific information about how and when to teach SC.

CHAPTER 7

# Teaching Sentence Combining

Maximizing the benefits of SC calls for frequent, systematic practice time within a writing curriculum. SC should not and cannot, however, replace the writing workshop as the primary method of instruction. Ideally, SC is best used as a skill-building addition to regular composition work (Strong, 1976) and as a complement to other research-validated writing practices.

Generally, SC exercises are best taught within a "learn–see–do" structure, with an emphasis on explicit modeling of the decisions students need to make when combining the kernel clusters, such as how and why to make various combinations. Teaching also needs to show the students how to combine sentences rather than telling them about SC. Students should practice with you before they write on their own. Feedback should be explicit, and practice sessions should be systematically provided so that SC skills are internalized. Although some students, including many students with writing disabilities, may need more instruction and guided practice, most students will take to the exercises naturally if you teach them in this manner.

## THE THREE SEGMENTS OF SENTENCE-COMBINING LESSONS

When you are first beginning to teach your class how to combine sentences, organize the lessons to include three critical segments: (1) teacher modeling, in which you demonstrate to the students what to do; (2) scaffolded practice, in which you guide students to develop multiple solutions to a problem; and (3) independent practice, in which the students create solutions to a problem, and these solutions are discussed and supportively evaluated by the whole class. (See Table 7.1.)

**TABLE 7.1. Critical Segments of a Typical Sentence-Combining Lesson**

1. Teacher modeling, in which you demonstrate to the students what to do.
2. Scaffolded practice, in which you guide students to develop multiple solutions to a problem.
3. Independent practice, in which the students create solutions to a problem that are discussed and supportively evaluated by the whole class.

SC exercises are best introduced to a class by explaining that this activity can help any writer create more interesting sentences that sound better to readers. Begin with whole-class discussion by showing students a simple pair of kernel sentences and modeling how they can possibly be combined; then share what your thinking was in performing the combination, and discuss why the new combination sounds better. The following teaching script is specific, yet generic enough to be effective at multiple levels. Always begin instruction with simple kernels placed so that students can read them easily, such as these:

The students are happy.
The students are smart.

Then begin to teach:

1. "Look at these two sentences." Read the sentences aloud.
2. "These sentences sound all right, but we can make them better."
3. "We are going to play with these sentences to make them sound better and more interesting. This play is called 'sentence combining.'"
4. "When we practice combining sentences, we will do these things:

   • Combine sentences together.
   • Change words or parts of sentences.
   • Add words or parts to the sentences.
   • Rearrange words or parts of sentences.
   • Delete words or parts of sentences."

   You may want to list these operations on a chart for reference.

5. "Learning how to combine sentences in different ways will help you write more interesting sentences that sound better to readers."
6. "Good writers often play with their sentences to make them sound better, just as we are going to do."
7. "One of the best parts about this activity is that there will usually be more than one solution to many of the practice problems."
8. "Look up here." Wait.

9. "Read the first sentence with me."

10. "Now read the second sentence with me."

11. "What is the new idea in the second sentence?" Wait for suggestions and then underline the new idea.

12. "I will combine this new idea into the first sentence to make one new sentence." Show the new sentence.

13. "Read the new sentence with me."

14. "This new sentence sounds good and makes sense."

15. "Remember how I said that one of the best parts about sentence combining is that there will usually be more than one solution to many of the practice problems?"

16. "Let me show you another way I could have combined the sentences." Show an alternative combination.

17. "How is this sentence different from the first sentence I made?" Wait.

18. "Let me show you one other way I could have combined the sentences." Show a second alternative combination.

19. "How is this sentence different from the first sentence I made?"

20. At this point, ask the students: "How exactly did I create the new sentence? How did I change the words around?" Wait. Then suggest that when combining sentences, you and they can do the following:

    - Combine the kernels in any grammatically acceptable sequence that sounds effective.
    - Change the form of words (e.g., *threw* to *was throwing*).
    - Add appropriate function words (e.g., *because, therefore, while, as soon as*).
    - Rearrange by moving words, phrases, and clauses around to produce the best effect.
    - Add or eliminate Details.

    Table 7.2 provides a mnemonic device, called C-CARD, to help you and your students remember the possible options when combining.

21. Show the students exactly where you performed each of those operations.

22. "When we combine sentences, you could use any or all of these operations when you make a new sentence."

23. Perform several more combinations while gradually asking students for input. Involve as many students in the process as you can by asking for specific ways to perform the C-CARD operations.

After modeling, the next instructional step is scaffolded practice, in which the students (either alone or in pairs) write out combinations for several additional kernel sentence clusters and then compare their solutions with yours. The final step is

**TABLE 7.2. Sentence-Combining Possibilities: C-CARD**

*Combine*
Combine the kernels in any grammatical acceptable sequence that sounds effective.

*Change*
Change the form of words (e.g., *threw* to *was throwing*).

*Add*
To add appropriate function words. For instance:
- *After,* as in *"After* the pitcher threw the ball, the batter swung the bat, hitting the ball high into the air."
- *As soon as,* as in "The batter swung the bat *as soon as* the pitcher threw the ball, hitting the ball high into the air."

*Rearrange*
Move parts around to change the sound or focus.

*Details*
Add or eliminate details. For example, adding *rapidly* to the batter's action creates "As the pitcher threw the ball, the batter *rapidly* swung the bat, hitting the ball high into the air." Adding *curving* to the pitcher's action adds a nice degree of detail: "As the pitcher threw the ball, the batter swung the bat, hitting the *curving* ball high into the air."

independent practice, where you assign a set of problems during class and the students write solutions, present them to their peers, and discuss them. Independent practice can also take the form of kernels assigned for homework, as long as the solutions are discussed in class.

Independent practice can be extended to the students' own writing by prompting them to use C-CARD to revise a current composition. Tell the students to highlight any changes that they make, so you can ensure that they are performing each element of the mnemonic.

There is no exact timetable for each of these steps. Depending on the students' skill level, it may take several lessons before they are comfortable with performing combinations independently. In addition, you may want to work in smaller groups or one on one with students who are struggling with acquiring the ability to combine sentences before you move on to independent practice.

## THE VALUE OF DISCUSSION

The two most important activities in SC are (1) the initial creation of a combination and (2) the discussion or evaluation of the combination. The practical and supportive discussions and comparisons of the constructions students generate from the kernel sentence exercises are the key to helping the students understand the possible options in revision. How much discussion is needed will depend on the age, maturity, and abilities of the students. You are likely to find that the more the students practice the exercises, the greater their ability to discuss the rhetorical effects of the solutions will be.

The exercises work very well within an environment of discovery. Therefore, it's best to create a classroom environment that encourages open discussion and community support—a place where everyone writes and where everyone is invested in everyone else's improvement. In this type of environment, student participation is essential. Students' gains will be directly proportional to the amount of their participation during the activities. Participation includes reading the exercises, writing solutions to the exercises, sharing responses with a partner or the class, and providing feedback on other students' responses.

## "MISTAKES"

During each of the lesson segments, encourage students not to worry about making "mistakes" when they change their sentences. When anyone is manipulating syntax, the mind is wrestling with thought. Therefore, we need to expect that students—particlarly those with weak backgrounds in reading or little practice in writing—will write many disastrous sentences before writing good ones (Strong, 1985). Explain that in these exercises they will be putting their words together into sentences in ways they never tried before, and that this is likely to require a bit of risk taking. Sometimes changes will make a sentence better; sometimes the changes will make the sentence worse. The point is that good writers try all sorts of combinations before discovering the best option, and that this process of discovery is exactly what they will be practicing during the exercises.

## ORAL PRACTICE

Most specific discussions and evaluations occur when sample student exercises are available to the whole class at once. (Daiker, Kerek, & Morenberg, 1979). However, it's also essential to present the exercises (and later compositions) orally as well as visually to all the students. The ear is an important element in deciding the effectiveness of a solution. Perhaps in your own writing you may read a section out loud to test the sound of the passage. Reading the exercise solutions aloud mimics this actual writing behavior. Reading sentences and compositions aloud should thus be included in each lesson, and students should be encouraged to try out the sound of alternative structures aloud during the composing process, as well as to transfer this skill from the exercises to actual writing (Neman, 1995).

Oral SC practice is effective in increasing syntactic fluency even without concurrent written practice (see Frank, 1993; Miller & Ney, 1968; Perron, 1974; Strong,

1976). Moreover, through oral practice, students learn to transfer their knowledge of oral language to writing (Strong, 1985).

Oral practice can follow an instruction sequence similar to that for written practice. For example, during the oral portion of a lesson, you can show students a set of kernel sentences and read the sentences out loud to the students. You can then model the first sentence combination, and next ask students in turn to provide other possible solutions. Write down the various combinations as the students provide them.

Oral practice can be incorporated into any practice time. Depending on your students' ability to transcribe their thoughts, you may choose to make a few practice sessions oral, to save time the students would otherwise spend on handwriting the new combinations.

## YOUR ROLE AS THE TEACHER DURING DISCUSSIONS

Consider your role as the teacher during the exercises as being more of a guide than a director. Initially you may need to teach students directly how and why to combine the kernels, but once students have acquired the "trick," allow the comments and conversations from the students to drive the lesson.

Your duty as the teacher is to initially create a series of sequenced exercises and then ask the kind of questions that will direct students' attention to the wide variety of syntactic options available to them in each rhetorical situation. Furthermore, your questions and guidance should help students formulate rhetorical guidelines for evaluating the relative merits of each option for the genre and the intended audience. Your praise should also be very specific. "Nice sentence" is far less effective praise for a new combination than "The new combination really does a great job of emphasizing the character's ideas" or "The rhythm of the new combination sounds so good when I read it." Specific praise about the particular aspects of the combined sentences that are effective may help students to understand the rhetorical effects and may increase the chance that they will make additional effective changes in the future. And, finally, you must help students to transfer the skills they have learned to real writing, or there will be little hope of their actually using these sentence-level skills to improve their prose.

Keep in mind these assumptions (based on Neman, 1995) when considering your role in discussion leadership and participation:

1.  Many students who are native speakers of English already have much of the linguistic decision-making ability they will need to make SC judgments intelligently. English language learners will benefit from the knowledge of their classmates.
2.  A positive, encouraging environment is the best learning environment. Emphasize strengths in the students' writing and abilities, rather than weaknesses. "Why do you think this version is better?" is a more effective

question, in terms of motivation, than "Why do you think this version is worse?"

3. The primary goal for these exercises is not to achieve "correctness"; it is to encourage syntactic and stylistic experimentation. You will encounter errors as students try out more complex constructions than they are accustomed to. Emphasizing correctness will probably cause many students to disengage from risk taking.

4. Initially, demonstrating a variety of options is more important to students' learning than closely evaluating and making judgments.

5. Since as few as five or six kernels can be combined into a very large number of quite grammatical constructions, there is rarely a single correct answer. There are variables that can be used to decide on correctness (and these are presented in Chapter 9 of this book), but keep in mind that even experts disagree about what might be considered "best" writing for a given situation.

## SCHEDULING PRACTICE SESSIONS

For many teachers, the main question about SC is not whether they should include such practice, but instead how exactly to fit these discussions into an already tight schedule of writing activities. Until the students are comfortable with the process of and rationale for SC, you will need to dedicate at least 30 minutes per session to SC exercises, to allow adequate time for the three segments of instruction discussed earlier in this chapter. However, after students can combine and discuss the combinations efficiently, the amount of time you will need to dedicate to the individual sessions can be reduced. The sessions need to be frequent, but they should not be long. Two or three times a week for short intervals at a time (approximately 10–20 minutes) will provide enough practice for most of the students in your classroom. Too much of even a very good thing can quickly reduce its potency. You can't allow yourself to become so enamored with the exercises that you allow other parts of your writing program to suffer.

Initially, you can use SC sessions as warm-ups for your regular writing workshop activities, or in place of other daily oral language practice you may already engage in. You can also use SC exercises as quick fill-ins between other instructional tasks by having students combine sentences in their writing journals.

## WHERE TO SCHEDULE SENTENCE COMBINING
## IN A WRITING WORKSHOP

During the writing process, SC exercises are best discussed and practiced when the students are revising. As discussed earlier, revising has been called a process of transforming sentences (Elbow, 1985). Presenting and discussing the exercises while students are revising written work may be the best time to help them transfer their newly gained sentence-transforming prowess to their actual writing. Since SC can help students understand such revision skills as expansion or reordering of ideas and tightening of language (Strong, 1985), it seems only logical to practice SC during the times in the writing process when these skills are most needed. Moreover, practicing SC during revising makes sense because young writers tend to have enough trouble simply getting their ideas onto the page in an initial draft; most don't or can't worry about polishing sentences during the first draft. You certainly do not want the focus on SC to interfere with the initial creation of thought. Sentence-revising work can occur later, when the ideas the students want to convey are more firmly in place. At that point, SC can help them refine and polish their message.

## SENTENCE-COMBINING BEST-PRACTICE SUGGESTIONS

One final thought for this chapter: SC exercises are effective, but if they are used ineffectively, their value will be reduced and precious learning time will be wasted. Hunt (1979), from his extensive experience with teaching and researching SC, offers several thoughts about the effective use of SC in the classroom. They are in a sense "best practices" in teaching SC, and as such make a nice conclusion to this chapter. In a classroom where SC is taught effectively, the following practices are seen:

1. Every SC exercise is a problem in expressing a prescribed thought in the best way—that is, using the most effective sentence structure.
2. Many students work on the same problem, investing their own time and thought. Consequently, they pay close attention; they care about whether their solutions are good ones; and they are interested in how their solutions differ from those of their peers.
3. Several solutions are presented for each problem. Class discussions are about better versus less effective solutions, rather than good versus bad or right versus wrong. Each student should see the various solutions and compare them.
4. Students make the judgments on solutions more often than you as the teacher do. This is good because:
   a. Students usually accept the judgments of their peers without the authority problem that a teacher's judgment might arouse.
   b. The students are more likely to care about the approval of their peers than about a teacher's approval.
   c. Students who offer judgments sense whether other students agree or disagree, and thus learn to make more accurate judgments about their own drafts. Such criticism of one's own work is an essential component of effective writing.
   d. An idiosyncratic judgment can be made by one person, including one teacher, but it is unlikely that the whole class will do so.

5. The subject matter of the exercises is age-appropriate and seems lively and interesting.
6. In making judgments on a student's solutions, everyone else accentuates the positive, not the negative.
7. The various solutions are discussed in depth as appropriate.

In the next chapter I discuss options for arranging the learning environment by using peer grouping and assistance.

CHAPTER 8

# Student Grouping

$S$C exercises can be implemented classwide or in small groups. Discussions of SC work well in a full-class setting, and you should certainly begin them this way. However, varying the instructional grouping arrangements by including peer-assisted practice is an effective way to differentiate instruction for students who may need additional support.

Unfortunately, when completing SC exercises, many students—especially those with disabilities in written expression—may only listen to the sound of their own voices when they combine their sentences. But often their sentences can be improved if other voices provide feedback on what they have written. Teachers can provide those other voices through writing conferences. However, teachers often cannot provide all of the feedback and reflection their students need for various reasons, including a lack of time, the numbers of students, and the level of support required by some students. If students are trained to provide support to one another through peer conferences, they can give and receive the feedback and support they need in a timelier and more effective manner.

## PEER CONFERENCING

When you are thinking beyond SC instruction to writing instruction in general, peer conferencing offers many advantages over large-group instruction. Wong (2000) describes peer conferencing as an interactive dialogue between writers. The external feedback gained through this type of interactive dialogue provides several important benefits to writers, especially those with disabilities. First, a writer who works with a peer can receive a direct response and feedback from a familiar audience (Stoddard & MacArthur, 1993) within a meaningful social context (Mac-Arthur, Schwartz, & Graham, 1991). Such conferences can help students reflect on their writing, realize dissonances, and create solutions (Wong, Butler, Ficzere, & Kuperis, 1996). The peer feedback gained through this type of grouping may even be more effective than teacher feedback in improving writing performance (Karegianes, Pascarella, & Pflaum, 1980). One reason for this is that students *believe* external feedback from peers improves their writing. For example, a child in a study designed to teach students writing in a peer-assisted format (Nixon & Topping, 2001) summarized his impressions of working with a peer by saying, "It was good because I wasn't on my own writing" (p. 52).

Encouraging children to work together may increase their overall interest in writing (Graham & Harris, 1997). Peer conferences may also increase overall writing ability, as working together increases response opportunities, which is an important factor associated with achievement (Brophy & Good, 1986). Through peer conferences, moreover, students can learn about different approaches and styles of writing, paving the way for the incorporation of new influences into their composing (McCutchen, 1988).

Discussing each other's writings also provides students with systematic opportunities to practice the important roles of author and editor. Through these opportunities, the students can learn to "see" their own thoughts and write from another's perspective (Wong et al., 1996). Peer conferencing also assists writers in the evaluation of problems they are encountering in their writing through extended practice in explicit discussions (Stoddard & MacArthur, 1993). Providing feedback on someone else's text may be a useful tool to increase students' awareness of the kinds of problems that can arise in written communication. Children also acquire self-regulatory skills through interaction with others during peer conferences (Zimmerman, 1989), as they observe and discuss how their peers successfully grapple with the complexities of writing.

In addition, any anxiety a writer may have about the conventions of writing (e.g., spelling and punctuation) may be lessened through conferencing with a peer, because the peer may be experiencing similar challenges with his or her own writing (Yarrow & Topping, 2001). Support from a peer who can honestly say, "I know what you mean. I have trouble with that too," may be just what some writers need to begin to increase their self-efficacy.

One area of writing where peer conferencing can be particularly influential is revising. Interestingly, students with the most minimal knowledge of revising may have the most to gain from conferencing (Fitzgerald & Stamm, 1992). Peer conferencing has been found to be effective in enhancing revisions—specifcally, the quantity of revisions (Saddler & Asaro, 2008; Fitzgerald & Stamm, 1990; MacArthur et al., 1991); the quality of rough drafts and finished pieces after revising (MacArthur et al., 1991; Olson, 1990); and clarity and cohesiveness after revising (Wong, Butler, Ficzere, Corden, & Zelmer, 1994).

Peer conferencing can also be a very effective method to help your students improve their SC ability (Saddler, Behforooz, & Asaro, 2008). In a peer setting, students can be asked to agree on a certain construction; this will compel the students to articulate why they prefer a given version over another. In addition, small peer groups are the natural context for oral SC exercises. The intimacy and interaction of a small-group setting make it ideal for orally reading and discussing syntactic options for written exercises—either ones you provide or examples taken from actual student prose.

Strong (1986) has described SC as an interactive form of sentence imitation and exploration—one that depends on language play and *immediate feedback*. He has further suggested that a classroom atmosphere of collaborative discussion replete with frequent opportunities for student response, such as would be created in a classroom employing peer grouping, is particularly well suited for the exploration of syntactic options. If a set of kernels can be solved in a peer situation, for example, the students can put that knowledge to work in their own writing. Asking peer groups to find solutions to problems can also help with team and classroom community building.

Remember that when you have peers work together, you must ensure that they are both engaged with the exercises. One way to do this is to have both create solutions to the exercises independently. Each student can then discuss his or her solution with the peer before the solutions are discussed in the whole-class setting.

## WONG'S PEER CONFERENCING ARRANGEMENT

There is no one correct way to arrange peer conferences; indeed, there are many options to choose from. One effective alternative for a peer conference is provided by Wong (2000). In Wong's version, two students will have a conference with the teacher. One student (the author) gives the other student (the critic) and the teacher a copy of his or her composition to read. While the critic and the teacher are reading, any area that is difficult to understand is underlined. The critic then asks the author to provide explanations and elaborations. The teacher prompts the critic to provide suggestions for improvements as well and may help the critic to articulate questions if needed. The teacher can also help the author by suggesting revision alternatives. When the critic is finished, the teacher may make suggestions for any problematic areas the critic may have missed during his or her critique. This cycle is then repeated, with the author and the critic switching roles. Finally, the students make the recommended revisions and return individually for a second conference with the teacher.

## PEER-ASSISTED LEARNING STRATEGIES

A second instructional arrangement, "peer-assisted learning strategies" (PALS), was specifically created to structure the learning environment to increase students' opportunities for active responding through collaborative practice (Greenwood,

Carta, & Kamps, 1990; Mathes & Fuchs, 1993; Fuchs, Fuchs, Mathes, & Simmons, 1997). PALS is a member of the collaborative learning family of instructional techniques, which in general give different groups of children opportunities to operate on varying levels of the curriculum simultaneously; such techniques thereby meet the needs of each student to a far greater degree than a typical lesson delivered in a large group can. PALS has been described as a promising alternative to conventional instructional methods (Fuchs & Fuchs, 2000).

In the early grades, a typical PALS lesson format involves pairing an academically stronger child with an academically weaker child from the same classroom. The stronger child is called the "coach" initially, and the weaker child is called the "player." Mathes and Fuchs (1993) suggest that when students are paired in such a manner, the stronger student takes on a teacher-like role and the weaker student benefits from having an appropriate model. Each pair then completes a tutoring routine that has been explicitly taught and modeled by the teacher. The tutoring routine may consist of the introduction of a skill, followed by practice and correction as needed. Generally the coach follows a written script to help deliver the instruction. The roles are later reversed, providing practice for the weaker student in monitoring and providing corrective feedback.

The use of a PALS format may be a particularly effective method to teach SC skills, as student pairs will have opportunities to create and discuss syntactic options. In particular, PALS can be incorporated with SC during the independent practice phase of a lesson. In this scheme the teacher provides two students' sets of kernel sentences to the students and explains that they will work as a team to figure out different fun ways to combine the sentences. As described above, the stronger student is initially designated as the coach and the other as the player. The coach uses a card with instructions printed on them. The instructions consist of the directions for how the sentences should be combined, and directions for the player's performance. The directions for the coach include telling the player to (1) read the sentences out loud; (2) decide the best way to combine the sentences; (3) write the answer on the sheet; and (4) read the new sentence. The coach then says "Good job" if the sentence is grammatical or "Almost" if the sentence is ungrammatical. If the sentence is ungrammatical, the coach provides suggestions on what changes to make in the sentence. If the coach cannot fix the sentence, the teacher provides assistance. After the sentence is written correctly, the roles are reversed, and the sequence is repeated until all sentences are completed. Once all kernel pairs are completed, each student reads a sentence to the teacher, who praises the effort and asks whether there is any other way that the sentence could have been combined.

Whether the Wong or the PALS arrangement is used, clearly peer practice offers enough potential advantages that it should be considered an essential element of SC instruction.

In the next chapter I discuss methods you can use to assess students' progress with SC.

CHAPTER 9

# Assessment

$A$ssessment is an important element of the teaching and learning process, because it is the only way we can determine whether our students are acquiring the skills we are teaching. Since SC exercises can be presented in a developmental sequence in terms of syntactic constructions (see Table 12.1 in Chapter 12, as well as Chapter 13), SC can be readily and systematically assessed. Assessment will differ depending on what is being checked, of course. The simple kernel sentence sets that are commonly used to introduce SC require a different type of assessment than a paragraph-length or whole-discourse-length exercise requires. However, through careful assessment, each step of your students' journey through the increasingly complex syntactic exercises can be carefully assessed. For example, you can assess whether your students can skillfully combine a set of kernels with and without cues. Furthermore, you can check to ensure that they can combine multiple kernels with and without cues. You will also want to assess to what extent your students' increased skill with combining sentences, as exhibited by better performance on the exercises, improves their writing. In other words, can students transfer the skills they are learning in the SC exercises to their connected writing activities?

Assessment is also important for students, because they will eventually want you to tell them whether their solutions are "better" than the other options presented during class discussions. Comparison is actually a very good thing and a natural and desirable outcome of instruction. As mentioned in Chapter 3, SC exercises, by presenting students with sets of simple sentences and requiring them to combine those sentences any way they wish as long as the product is grammatically correct, allow for the possibility of more than one "right" answer. The fact that there can be acceptable alternatives should be emphasized and can become itself a subject of instruction (Nutter & Safran, 1984).

## GRADING'S EFFECT ON LEARNING ENVIRONMENTS

Before I discuss the types of assessment that can be used to measure progress in SC, it may be helpful to summarize the importance of the learning environment in which the exercises are taught. The most effective environment for learning and practicing SC occurs when the exercises are presented as puzzles to be solved and the solutions are reached in a playful, exploratory atmosphere. In this environment, the emphasis during practice sessions should never be on being "right" or "wrong." If a response is ungrammatical, or less grammatically effective than other responses, then the emphasis should be on improving the response through problem-solving different alternatives.

Grading can have a dramatic impact on such an environment. Theoretically, you should not "grade" the exercises. Grading the practice work might attach risk to the exercises in the students' minds. To be most effective, SC exercises must be without risk; that is, they must allow students to experiment with syntactic structures without fear of being incorrect. However, because you are investing time in teaching SC, you will want to know whether your students are making progress with the exercises. In addition, the students will want to know how they are doing.

## FOUR COMPARATIVE METRICS

Through SC practice sessions and discussions, students will realize that some solutions are better than others, and may want to know what criteria they can use to differentiate the best combinations. There are three metrics that can be used to make comparisons—grammaical correctness, analytic scoring factors (punctuation, capitalization, and use of target structures), and effectiveness—and a fourth metric that should never be used. Let's discuss the fourth metric, which is sentence length, first.

Sentence length is not a useful metric because length alone does not automatically equal improved quality. For example, take the following sentence:

> I like the movie we saw about Moby Dick the white whale the captain said if you can kill the white whale Moby Dick I will give this gold to the one that can do it and it is worth sixteen dollars they tried and tried but while they were trying they killed a whale and used the oil for the lamps they almost caught the white whale.

If you had suggested to your students that the best combination is the longest, then this solution would be one of the best in the class! However, this sentence is clearly problematic.

## Grammatical Correctness

Grammatical correctness is the first metric a solution can effectively be measured against. This metric is a simple one: A solution is incorrect if it does not conform to grammatical rules, and correct if the rules are followed.

A word of caution about grammatical correctness is in order, however. Although our language does have rules governing syntax, engaging students in the grammatical explanation of why a solution is correct or incorrect may not be productive. Depending on your students' abilities, complex grammatical terminology may not help them understand how to improve their work. In fact, belaboring grammatical terminology may only confuse students.

When you are using grammatical correctness as a metric, you can administer a probe containing 5 or 10 kernel sentence problems. Scoring this type of exercise can be very simple; for example, if the sentences are grammatically correct, then the solutions are correct. However, some teachers post or pass out possible solutions for the problems and require students to check their sentences against the key. Figure 9.1 is a quiz that was used to check progress after a unit of instruction. If the students combined the sentences in a grammatically correct way and each sentence contained all of the important information from the kernels, the solutions were correct.

This type of probe is useful for assessing students' knowledge before SC instruction begins; it can also be used as a quick progress-monitoring check of the constructions being taught. Although it is simple, a probe such as this offers quick feedback of students' ability to manipulate syntax. Naturally, if the students are working through cued exercises, the combinations will not only have to be grammatically correct, but will also have to contain the cue word in the solution. These types of probes should not be a major factor in the overall writing grade a student achieves in your course. They represent one source of data on the acquisition of one writing skill. Nevertheless, they are still useful in helping you gauge the effectiveness of your instruction.

## Analytic Scoring Factors

In addition to grammatical correctness, punctuation, capitalization, and the use of target structures can be used to score SC exercises.

Punctuation and capitalization can be checked through a simple analysis: Compare the number of instances of punctuation and capitalization a solution should have with each student's actual work. If the solution should have included four elements and the student only included three, the score would be 3 of 4, or 75%. An example for this type of scoring is provided below:

> *Kernels:*    Sue has a red car.
> The car is a Chevy.
> Steve has a blue car.

The car is a Ford.
Dave has a yellow car.
The car is a Dodge.

One possible combination for these sentences is this:

Sue has a red Chevy, Steve has a blue Ford, and Dave has a yellow Dodge.

This combination includes 6 capital letters and 3 punctuation marks, for a total of 9 instances. If a student produced this solution—

Sue has a red Chevy steve has a blue Ford and Dave has a yellow Dodge.

—his or her score would be 6 out of 9, or 66%, because the student failed to include capitalization and punctuation elements.

---

**Name:** _____          **Date:** _____

1.  The gorilla ran.
    The gorilla was huge.
    He ran out of the cage.

    _____

    _____

2.  The zookeeper stared.
    He stared at the gorilla.
    His mouth was open.

    _____

    _____

3.  The girl grabbed the ball.
    She was on the chair.
    She grabbed it with her hand.

    _____

    _____

4.  The teacher was writing.
    The writing was on the chalkboard.
    She wrote with blue chalk.

    _____

    _____

---

**FIGURE 9.1.** Sentence-combining unit quiz.

Although punctuation and capitalization are easy enough to score, the use of target structures requires explanation. To use this method effectively, analyze a sample of each student's writing for the target SC construction that will be taught in an upcoming unit. Then, after the construction is taught, encourage students to include that particular construction in future writings. When you are scoring their writing, include a category on a scoring rubric that assesses the use of the target structures. This scoring method may serve to promote transfer and generalization of these structures from the exercises to the students' actual writing.

## Effectiveness

Although grammatical correctness, capitalization, punctuation, and target structures can all be used to assess SC, sentence combinations must pass a higher standard: effectiveness. Effectiveness relies on two factors—the ear and the intent of the writer. If a sentence is not grammatically correct, the ear should be able to pick up the resounding dissonance of the nongrammatical clunker. For example, if a student writes the sentence *The was dog happy,* the error is likely to be discovered when the sentence is read aloud, without a need to diagram the proper arrangements of nouns and verbs within a sentence. Likewise, if a writer pens the sentence *The dog were happy,* the noun–verb agreement hitch will probably be discovered without an extended technical discussion.

Effectiveness is a better metric than grammar, however, because a grammatically correct sentence can often still be improved. In other words, a sentence can be grammatically correct, but may still not be written in the most effective manner. If a sentence is grammatically correct, then effectiveness becomes an issue of which sounds better, given the rhetorical situation, the writer's intent, and the reader's needs. Unfortunately, effectiveness is more difficult to measure than grammatical correctness, because there is no finite set of rules governing what makes a sentence effective.

Effectiveness is literally producing an intended or expected result and/or making a deep or vivid impression. In SC, the most effective solution is one that (1) sounds good to the ear and (2) matches the intent of the writer, given the rhetorical situation and the reader's needs.

Focusing on effectiveness provides support for the important reality that in SC exercises there will rarely be a right versus a wrong answer; instead, there will be some sentence combinations that simply sound better or are more effective representations of the writer's intent than others. When you are gauging effectiveness, the message to students must be "That's right, but there might be a better way to say it." Emphasizing effectiveness in this way will prompt students to understand that often in writing there is no one right answer, no one right way to form an idea. Rather, there may be multiple solutions that require introspection before the best option is selected.

Gauging effectiveness also encourages risk taking, as it welcomes "mistakes" as opportunities for problem solving. Within this context, "mistakes" become sentences that can be formed in better ways than the writer originally attempted. This concept may be especially beneficial for less skilled writers, who are often unwilling to take risks within their writing.

The question then becomes how to gauge effectiveness. What criteria should be used? And how can you best teach what makes one sentence more effective than another?

Neman (1995) recommends three standards to aid students in gauging the effectiveness of solutions: (1) clarity and directness of meaning, (2) rhythmic appeal, and (3) intended audience. Clearly, all of these standards are highly subjective.

## Teaching and Assessing Effectiveness

Begin the process of comparison after students are comfortable with combining two kernel sentences in multiple ways. Place sets of three or more kernel sentences so all students can see them. For example:

> The pitcher threw the ball.
> The batter swung the bat.
> The bat hit the ball.
> The ball went high into the air.

Then read the following script:

1. "Let's look at this group of sentences. Follow along as I read them to you." Read the sentences.
2. "One possible combination of these kernel sentence clusters might be: *After the pitcher threw the ball, the batter swung the bat, hitting the ball high into the air.*"
3. "But this might not be the 'best' combination. The only way to tell if this is the most effective combination is to test it against other options."
4. "Let's look at two other options, and then let's discuss which one we like the best and why." Have two other combinations already prepared. One of these alternatives should be combined in a way that does not sound as good as the original, and the other should be a very basic way to combine the original sentences. Therefore, you will end up with a highly effective combination, a good combination, and a not-so-good combination. See Figure 9.2 for examples. Show each and read to students.
5. "Which combination sounds best? Why?"
6. "Which seems the clearest and most direct (easiest to understand)? Why?"
7. "Which would be the best if you were writing to a friend? Which might be best if you were writing to me? Why?"
8. "The way we are discussing these combinations is the same way we will discuss the solutions we compare in class, and the same way I will use when I score your combinations that you give me."

A. The pitcher threw the ball and the batter swung and the bat hit the ball and the ball went high into the air.

B. After the pitcher threw the ball, the batter swung the bat, hitting the ball high into the air.

C. The batter swung the bat after the pitcher threw the ball, hitting the ball into the air very high.

**FIGURE 9.2.** Options for evaluating effectiveness of sentence combinations.

Applying Neman's (1995) three standards to these possible solutions through discussion might lead your students to suggest that solution B in Figure 9.2 is the most direct, clear, and rhythmical, and solution A the least so. Or students could vote solution B to be the best for an intended audience of adults, or solution A for an audience of their peers. Naturally, there could be disagreement as to which sentence best meets which standard, but that is the whole point. When students compare different solutions to the same problem through discussion, they can develop a better sense of how effectiveness might be perceived by different readers. These discussions may also help the students to become more confident in their own ability to make effective decisions in crafting and revising their own texts.

It is also helpful to practice making comparisons by using passages from authors the students are familiar with. Through discussion, the class can consider why these passages are clear and direct, or why the rhythm sounds good to the ear, or how the intended audience is well served by the way the author presents ideas. However, when instruction has progressed to paragraph-length exercises, the gauging of effectiveness becomes more complex, as context becomes the prime consideration.

In connected text, the "goodness" or "quality" of a sentence depends on how well that sentence functions and supports the other sentences within that paragraph—and, in a broader sense, on how well the sentence supports the overall goal of the composition. Although these criteria are more complex, applying Neman's (1995) standards to paragraph-length exercises can help the criteria become more understandable to the students, because the standards can only be truly appreciated when they are applied to specific writing situations. Sentence length, syntactic arrangement, vocabulary, and ideation are all dependent on the rhetorical situation. For instance, a short sentence positioned at the end of a paragraph containing long, complex sentences may serve nicely to emphasize a key point. Consider this example:

What's more important still is the issue of a double ration of smokes. Ten cigars, twenty cigarettes, and two quids of chew per man; now that is decent. I have exchanged my chewing tobacco with Katczinsky for his cigarettes, which means I have forty altogether. That's enough for a day. (Remarque, 1929/1982, p. 2)

Likewise, a short sentence to begin a paragraph may have a similar effect, as in this example:

It is autumn. There are not many of the old hands left. I am the last of the seven fellows from class. (Remarque, 1929/1982, p. 293).

To help students score qualitative effectiveness on paragraph- and whole-discourse-length pieces, discussion becomes paramount. One way to start such a discussion is to have student pairs read two versions of the same piece of writing. Prompt your students to read through the paragraph quickly first, to gain an overall impression. Suggest that they try to answer the overall question "Which version is better?" after they first scan the paragraph. After they have determined which version is "better," ask them how they determined the winner. What criteria did they use? After hearing (and recording) their responses, model how Neman's (1995) standards can be used. After formulating an opinion of the overall quality of the piece, you can look at the individual parts. For example, you can apply Neman's standards to the introduction, the body, and the conclusions.

To further explain Neman's (1995) standards, you can develop evaluative questions that students can use to discuss the effectiveness of the piece. Here is one example of such a set of questions:

1. Which of the two versions do you think is better? Why?
2. In what major ways do the versions differ?
   a. Which begins better?
   b. Which has the more logical organization?
   c. Which has the more effective conclusion?
3. Which version seems to be more understandable to you? Why?
4. Which version do you believe the intended audience will enjoy more? Why?
5. Which version offers more variety in sentence structure?
6. Which has included the more remarkable or interesting structures?
7. Which is the more rhythmically effective version? How is this effectiveness achieved?

Once students are comfortable with using these questions to examine others' work, have them apply the questions to their own pieces. To help them with scoring, a rubric based on Neman's standards is presented in Figure 9.3, while two additional examples of questionnaires that students could use to discuss and rate each other's compositions are provided in Figures 9.4 and 9.5. Each of these figures offers a set of questions to guide students' qualitative analysis of each other's writing pieces. They also prompt the students to check for either SC specifically, or the quality of sentences more generally.

---

1. **Meaning.** As far as you can determine, have you conveyed the idea intended by the original author? A sentence should express a more or less complete thought, and extra meaning comes from the particular context in which the sentence is written or spoken.

2. **Clarity.** Is the sentence clear? Can it be understood on the first reading? An important characteristic of a speech or prose composition is that it communicates effectively with its intended audience. In general, the qualities of clearly written prose include a carefully defined purpose, logical organization, well-constructed sentences, and precise word choice.

3. **Coherence.** Do the various parts of the sentence fit together logically and smoothly?

4. **Emphasis.** Are key words and phrases put in emphatic positions (usually at the very end or at the very beginning of the sentence)?

5. **Conciseness.** Does the sentence clearly express an idea without wasting words? Concise writing is generally free of repetition and needless details.

6. **Rhythm.** Does the sentence flow, or is it marked by awkward interruptions? Do the interruptions help to emphasize key points (an effective technique), or do they merely distract (an ineffective technique)? The word *rhythm* comes from the Greek, meaning "flow."

---

**FIGURE 9.3.** A general rubric for effectiveness. Based on Neman (1995).

A final thought: When you and your students are discussing the effectiveness of various combinations, there are no hard rules or answers. Instead, think of the act of comparison as valuable in and of itself. Through such comparisons, young writers can begin to consider what style of writing they like and how effective writing sounds. Both are important considerations when they begin to craft their own prose.

The next chapter includes a sample unit of instruction, including lessons, worksheets, and assessments.

**Author's Name:** _____

**Title of Work:** _____

**Date of Draft:** _____

**Number of Draft:** _____

**Directions:** Use the following guide while you read the rough draft. Put as much detail as you can into each question. The more comments, the better the work will become. Make sure you include any questions you have for the author. Use the back of the sheet if you need more space to write.

What made the story interesting?

What were the characters like?

How was the setting unique?

Was the ending what you expected?

What did you like best about the story?

What was the most exciting part of the story?

What part of the story do you want to know more about?

Was the story organized and easy to follow?

Did the author use a variety of different sentences?

What vivid vocabulary did the author use?

**Peer Editor:** _____

**FIGURE 9.4.** Student Questionnaire 1.

**Author's Name:** _____

**Title of Work:** _____

**Directions:** Answer the following questions while you read your partner's story. Give your partner as many good ideas as you can. The more ideas, the better the revised story will be.

What did you like about the characters?

What made the setting fun?

What made the ending fun?

What did you like best about the story?

What part of the story do you want to know more about?

Where did the author use the sentence-combining tricks? Circle the sentences in the story.

What sentences can the author change to make the story more interesting? Put an "×" above the sentence in the story.

**Peer Editor:** _____

**FIGURE 9.5.** Student Questionnaire 2.

# PART III

# SAMPLE UNIT OF INSTRUCTION, PRACTICE ACTIVITIES, AND EXERCISES

CHAPTER 10

# Sample Unit of Instruction

In this chapter an SC unit previously taught to second-grade students with writing disabilities (see Saddler & Graham, 2005) is provided to demonstrate how a sequence of SC lessons can flow together. The topic of the unit was creating compound sentences by using the connectors *and, but, because*. All of the prompts and charts used during instruction are provided, and each lesson has been completely scripted.

In this unit, the first three lessons include these components: (1) review of the prior lesson and activation of prior knowledge (except for the first lesson in the unit), and prediction about what the exercise will be about, based on its title; (2) introduction and explanation of the new SC topic; (3) oral warm-up, during which the students apply the topic by combining sets of two kernel sentences printed on paper; (4) written practice in combining sets of kernel sentences under your direction; (5) written independent practice in a peer-mediated format; (6) summary; and (7) preview of the next lesson.

## LESSON 1

**Materials:** Good Sentence Chart (Figure 10.1), sentence examples (Figure 10.2), warm-up sentences (Figure 10.3), kernel sentences (Figure 10.4), PAL practice sentences (Figure 10.5), and Coaching Card (Figure 10.6).

**Purpose:** Introduction of concepts (good sentences and SC); connecting sentences with *and, but, because.*

79

**Introduction**

1. Say, "We are going to spend some time playing with sentences. I am going to show you a trick that good writers use to write good sentences. Good writers often play with their sentences to make them sound better. Sometimes they may change some words, move some words around, add some words, or take out words. This trick is called 'sentence combining.' We are going to use sentence combining to change sentences around to make them sound better, just like good writers do. You are really going to enjoy the activities we do together, because playing with sentences can be a lot of fun. These activities will help you become a better writer. Today we are going to work with sentences I have written, but later on we will be working with sentences you write."

2. Ask, "What makes a good sentence?"

3. Lead them to the idea that a good sentence can be one that (show them the Good Sentence Chart [Figure 10.1] and discuss):

   a. Is easy for the reader to understand.

   b. Uses the right words to tell the reader exactly what your idea is and something about that idea.

   c. Expresses your idea in a fun, interesting way that the reader will enjoy.

4. Ask, "Can you tell a good sentence when you hear one?"

5. Show them these examples (from Figure 10.2):

   > The bus stops.
   > The children get off.
   > The children go into school.
   > The children go to the classrooms.

6. Ask, "Are these sentences good?"

7. Ask, "What makes them good?"

---

A good sentence . . .

☺ Is easy for the reader to understand.

☺ Uses the right words to tell the reader exactly what your idea is and something about that idea.

☺ Expresses your idea in a fun, interesting way that the reader will enjoy.

---

**FIGURE 10.1.** Good Sentence Chart.

The bus stops.

The children get off.

The children go into school.

The children go to the classrooms.

**FIGURE 10.2.** Lesson 1 sentence examples.

8. Ask, "How could we make them better?"

9. Suggest, "One way these sentences could be more interesting for a reader is if we changed them around a little, because they all sound alike. Also, short sentences like these are sometimes not as easy for the reader to understand."

10. Say, "Let's look at the first two sentences and see if we could change them from two short, simple sentences into one sentence that is easier to understand."

11. Lead students to combine the sentences. Praise their effort.

12. Explain, "The way we played with these sentences—changig them, putting them together, adding words if we wanted, and taking other words out—is what we are going to start practicing together."

13. Say, "The point of sentence-combining practice is to get better at moving sentence parts around."

14. Ask them how such practice might help them in real writing. Reinforce the idea that being better at writing sentences frees the mind to focus on planning (thinking about what you will say) and organization (putting your ideas in order).

**Warm-Up**

15. Say, "Each day we will start with a few sentences as warm-ups. We will do the warm-ups out loud. Then we will learn a new way to change sentences, and you will get to change some sentences on paper first with me and then with each other."

16. Say, "There are all kinds of ways good writers combine sentences. Today we will start to learn how to put sentences together with words you can use to stick two short sentences together. These words will help you write your sentences in different ways and will help make your sentences more interesting."

17. Set out the warm-up sentence sheet for this lesson (Figure 10.3). Cover all but the first set of sentences. Read the first sentence and model how to combine. Then explain how the word in parentheses is a clue they can use to put the two short sentences together. Explain that the words that are underlined must be

1. Tom is Billy's friend.
   Joe is Billy's friend. (and)

2. They wanted Billy to eat worms.
   Billy did not want to eat worms. (but)

3. They wanted to find big worms.
   They wanted to make Billy sick. (because)

4. Tom got a shovel.
   Joe got a shovel. (and)

5. They started to dig under a tree in the apple orchard.
   The ground was too hard. (but)

6. They went to the creek.
   The ground was soft by the creek. (because)

**FIGURE 10.3.** Lesson 1 warm-up sentences. (The sentences here and in Figures 10.4–10.5 are from *How to Eat Fried Worms* by Thomas Rockwell, 1973.)

included in the new sentence. Then ask for a volunteer to read the next pair of sentences aloud. Ask for ideas on how to put the sentences together by using the clue. Praise the effort. (If the volunteer cannot provide an example, ask another student. If both are stuck, provide an example and move to the next pair of sentences.)

18. Write down one really good example from each student.
19. Finish the warm-up sentences.
20. Ask the students, "How are we able to do what we've been doing? How do we know how to put the sentences together?" Prompt them to say that we do it by:
    a. Using connecting words (words that help fit two sentences together).
    b. Getting rid of words we don't need.
    c. Moving words around.
    d. Changing some words (word endings).
    e. Adding words if we want to.
21. Show them where they did some of these different operations in the sentence they wrote.

**Directed Practice**

22. Say, "The point of sentence-combining practice is to get better at moving sentence parts around."

23. Ask students how such practice might help in real writing situations.

24. Say, "You already know a lot about how to put sentences together. Let's start to learn and practice writing out some different combinations."

25. Give each student a sheet of notebook paper and a pencil. Have each student place name and date on the sheet.

26. Show students the first sentence from the kernel sentence practice sheet for this lesson (Figure 10.4). Cover the remainder of the sentences on the sheet.

27. Have a volunteer read the first kernel sentence pair.

28. Discuss how the words in italics (*and, but, because*) can help students put short sentences together. (If a situation where a student uses *and, and, and, and* over and over as connectors does not come up, suggest that this type of writing is what young writers do, but that older writers don't do this because it is not very interesting.)

29. Prompt for ways to combine the kernel sentences aloud. Accept all grammatically correct options. Prompt the students to say how the sentences sounded to them. Use a system of hand cues: If a sentence sounds really great, give it a *thumbs-up*; if it sounds OK, put your *thumb parallel* with the ground. The trick is to get students to defend their opinions. If a student provides an ungrammatical sentence, ask whether the sentence sounds right. Don't try to explain the technicalities; try to get them to rely on their own knowledge of language. Say that it is OK to make mistakes because we learn from our mistakes. Encourage them to take risks. Then ask for ways to make the sentence sound better. Direct each student to write on his or her paper one combined sentence the student has suggested orally. Read the sentences out loud again when the students are finished.

---

1. Tom made a bet with Billy.
   Joe made a bet with Billy. (and)

2. Billy would win $50.
   Billy had to eat 15 worms. (but)

3. Tom said be needed to eat 15 worms.
   Tom didn't think Billy could eat that many. (because)

4. Tom had to find the worms.
   Joe had to find the worms. (and)

5. They found 10 worms near the pond.
   They still needed 5 more worms. (but)

---

**FIGURE 10.4.** Lesson 1 kernel sentence practice.

30. For the remainder of the kernel sentence pairs, have the students continue to provide oral suggestions for combinations before writing one answer on their paper. Read the sentences out loud again when the students are finished. Provide support as needed.

**PALS Practice**

31. Bring out the PALS practice sheet for this lesson (Figure 10.5).

32. Say, "Now you will try some sentences together without my help. When you work together as a team to practice combining the sentences, sometimes one of you will be the coach and the other will be the player. I will show you what the coach will do. The coach will read this Coaching Card (show them the Coaching Card [Figure 10.6]) to the player. This card tells the coach what to do. The coach will use a sheet of paper to cover all but the first set of sentences. Then the coach will read the directions on the card to the player. The directions say, 'Read both sentences out loud. Use the sentence-combining trick we are learning to make one new sentence out loud. If the sentence is not a thumbs-up, we will fix the sentence together. If the sentence is a thumbs-up, write the sentence on your paper.' After the player writes the sentence, the coach will move the paper down to show the next pair when the player is finished with the first pair."

33. Pick the higher-performing child in each pair to be the coach first. Have the coach read the Coaching Card, and then ask that child to start.

34. *Briefly* discuss the coach's answer after each problem. If the sentence is a thumbs-down, prompt the coach to try to fix it. If the coach gets stuck, provide an example. Suggest that the new combination is much more interesting and easier to

---

1. They found five worms under a tree stump.
   Joe dug a hole under a tree stump. (because)

2. Billy had to eat a worm every day.
   Billy had to eat every bit of the worm. (and)

3. The first worm was big.
   The other worms were bigger. (but)

4. Joe wanted to find even bigger worms.
   Joe wanted Billy to lose the bet. (because)

5. Joe dipped a worm in cornmeal.
   Joe put the worm in a frying pan. (and)

---

**FIGURE 10.5.** Lesson 1 PALS practice.

---

1. Read both sentences out loud.

2. Use the sentence-combining trick we are learning to make one new sentence out loud.

3. If the sentence is not a thumbs-up, we will fix the sentence together.

4. If the sentence is a thumbs-up, write the sentence on your paper.

---

**FIGURE 10.6.** Coaching Card.

understand. Ask whether there is any other way the sentences could have been combined. Then prompt to continue.

35. After finishing the first half of the problems, have students switch roles and repeat the procedure.

36. When the students are finished, praise the effort.

37. Say, "Today we worked on combining sentences by using words that can connect two short sentences. These words made the sentences you wrote easier to understand and more interesting."

38. Say, "I want you to try to use this trick you have learned to combine sentences in your regular classroom or anywhere else when you are not with me. You can use the trick when you are talking or when you are writing sentences. Tomorrow I will ask you what you used the trick for."

39. Say, "Next lesson we will work with different and longer sentences."

## LESSON 2

**Materials:** Good Sentence Chart (Figure 10.1), sentence examples (Figure 10.7), warm-up sentences (Figure 10.8), kernel sentences (Figure 10.9), PALS practice sentences (Figure 10.10), and Coaching Card (Figure 10.6).

**Purpose:** Reviewing concepts (good sentences and SC); connecting sentences with *and, but, because.*

### Introduction

1. Say, "Today we are going to spend some time again playing with sentences. Before we begin, did you have a chance to use this trick for any sentences you wrote? Tell me about it." Prompt students for responses.

2. Say, "Remember, I said we will be practicing a trick that good writers use to write good sentences. Good writers often play with their sentences to make them sound better. Sometimes they may change some words, add some words, or they may take out words. Can anyone tell me the name of this trick? This trick is called 'sentence combining.' We are going to use sentence combining to change sentences around to make them sound better, just like good writers do. Remember, try to use the trick when you write. It will help you become a better writer. Today we are going to work with sentences I have written, but later on we will be working with sentences you write."

3. Ask, "What makes a good sentence?"

4. Lead them to the ideas shown in the Good Sentence Chart (Figure 10.1) and discuss.

5. Ask, "Can you tell a good sentence when you hear one?"

6. Show them these new sentence examples (from Figure 10.7):

    a. The bell rings.

    b. The children stand up.

    c. The children go into the hallway.

    d. The children go to the lunchroom.

7. Ask, "Are these sentences good?"

8. Ask, "What makes them good?"

9. Ask, "How could we make them better?"

10. Suggest, "One way these sentences could be more interesting for a reader is if we changed them around a little because they all sound alike. Also, that short sentences like these are sometimes not as easy for the reader to understand."

11. Say, "Let's look at the first two sentences and see if we could change them from two short simple sentences into one sentence that is easier to understand."

12. Lead students to combine the sentences. Praise their effort.

13. Ask if they could add any words (description words or action helpers—give

---

The bell rings.

The children stand up.

The children go into the hallway.

The children go to the lunchroom.

---

**FIGURE 10.7.** Lesson 2 sentence examples.

examples) to the sentences that would help the reader understand the ideas any better. Praise the effort.

14. Explain, "The way we played with these sentences—changig them, putting them together, adding words if we wanted, and taking other words out—is what we are going to start practicing together." Be specific in your praise about what you like in the sentence.

15. Ask, "What is the point of sentence-combining practice?" (Elicit: To get better at moving sentence parts around.)

16. Ask them how such practice might help them in real writing. Reinforce the idea that being better at writing sentences will free their minds to focus on planning (thinking about what they will say) and organization (putting their ideas in order).

**Warm-Up**

17. Say, "Today we will start with a few sentences as warm-ups. We will do the warm-ups out loud. Then we will practice a new way to change sentences, and you will get to change some sentences on paper first with me and then with each other."

18. Say, "There are all kinds of ways good writers combine sentences. Does anyone remember how we combined the sentences the last lesson? Today we will continue to practice how to put sentences together with words you can use to stick two short sentences together. These words will help you write your sentences in different ways and will help make your sentences more interesting."

19. Set out the warm-up sentence sheet for this lesson (Figure 10.8). Cover all but the first set of sentences. Read the first sentence and model how to combine. Then explain how the word in parentheses is a clue they can use to put the two short sentences together. Explain that the words that are underlined must be included in the new sentence. Then ask for a volunteer to read the next pair of sentences aloud. Ask for ideas on how to put the sentences together by using the clue. Praise the effort. (If the volunteer cannot provide an example, ask another student. If both are stuck, provide an example and move to the next pair of sentences.)

20. Write down one really good example from each student.

21. Finish the warm-up sentences.

22. Ask the students, "How are we able to do what we've been doing? How do we know how to put the sentences together?" Prompt them to say that we do it by:

    a. Using connecting words (words that help fit two sentences together).

    b. Getting rid of words we don't need.

    c. Moving words around.

1. They looked under some flat rock.
   They found a huge night crawler. (and)

2. They tried to put the worm in their bag.
   The worm did not fit in their bag. (but)

3. Joe had to carry the worm in his hands.
   Joe carried the worm because the worm was very large. (because)

4. Joe went to Billy's house.
   Tom went to Billy's house. (and)

**FIGURE 10.8.** Lesson 2 warm-up sentences. (The sentences here and in Figures 10.9–10.10 are again from *How to Eat Fried Worms* by Thomas Rockwell, 1973).

    d. Changing some words (word endings).

    e. Adding words if we want to.

23. Show them where they did some of these different operations in the sentences they wrote.

**Directed Practice**

24. Say, "Remember, the point of sentence-combining practice is to get better at moving sentence parts around."

25. Ask students how such practice might help in real writing situations.

26. Say, "When writers get better at writing really good, interesting sentences, their minds are free to think about what they want to Say, and how to make their story better."

27. Say, "You already know a lot about how to put sentences together. Let's start to learn and practice writing out some different combinations."

28. Give each student a sheet of notebook paper and a pencil. Have each student place name and date on the sheet.

29. Show students the first sentence from the kernel sentence practice sheet (Figure 10.9). Cover the remainder of the sentences on the sheet.

30. Have a volunteer read the first kernel sentence pair.

31. Discuss how the words in italics (*and, but, because*) can help students put short sentences together.

32. Prompt for ways to combine the kernel sentences aloud. Accept all grammatically correct options. Prompt the students to say how the sentences sounded to them. As in Lesson 1, use a system of hand cues: If a sentence sounds really great, give

1. Joe brought the worm to Billy on a plate.
   Billy wanted ketchup and mustard. (but)

2. Billy wanted to cover up the taste of the worm.
   The worm tasted squishy. (because)

3. Billy put ketchup on the worm.
   Billy put mustard on the worm. (and)

4. Billy put the worm on his fork.
   Billy couldn't put it in his mouth. (but)

5. Billy had to close his eyes.
   Billy could not look at the worm on his fork. (because)

**FIGURE 10.9.** Lesson 2 kernel sentence practice.

it a *thumbs-up*; if it sounds OK, put your *thumb parallel* with the ground. The trick is to get students to defend their opinions. If a student provides an ungrammatical sentence, ask whether the sentence sounds right. Don't try to explain the technicalities; try to get them to rely on their own knowledge of language. Say that it is OK to make mistakes because we learn from our mistakes. Encourage them to take risks. Then ask for ways to make the sentence sound better. Direct each student to write on his or her paper one combined sentence the student has suggested orally. Read the sentences out loud again when the students are finished.

33. For the remainder of the kernel sentence pairs, have the students continue to provide oral suggestions for combinations before writing one answer on their paper. Read the sentences out loud again when the students are finished. Provide support as needed.

**PALS Practice**

34. Bring out the PALS practice sheet for this lesson (Figure 10.10).

35. Say, "Now you will try some sentences together without my help. When you work together as a team to practice combining the sentences, sometimes one of you will be the coach and the other will be the player. I will show you what the coach will do. The coach will read this coaching card (show them the Coaching Card [Figure 10.6]) to the player. This card tells the coach what to do. The coach will use a sheet of paper to cover all but the first set of sentences. Then the coach will read the directions on the card to the player. The directions say, 'Read both sentences out loud. Use the sentence-combining trick we are learning to make

1.  Billy shut his eyes.
    Billy put the worm in his mouth. (and)

2.  The worm was squishy.
    The worm did not taste bad. (but)

3.  Billy did not mind the taste.
    Billy could only taste the ketchup and mustard. (because)

4.  Billy ate the rest of the worm.
    Billy put his fork down. (and)

5.  Billy ate the worm.
    Billy could not think about eating another worm. (but)

**FIGURE 10.10.**  Lesson 2 PALS practice.

one new sentence out loud. If the sentence is not a thumbs-up, we will fix the sentence together. If the sentence is a thumbs-up, write the sentence on your paper.' After the player writes the sentence, the coach will move the paper down to show the next pair when the player is finished with the first pair and read the directions again."

36. Pick the higher-performing child in each pair to be the coach first. Have the coach read the Coaching Card, and then ask that child to start.

37. *Briefly* discuss the coach's answer after each problem. If the sentence is a thumbs-down, prompt the coach to try to fix it. If the coach gets stuck, provide an example. Suggest that the new combination is much more interesting and easier to understand. Ask whether there is any other way the sentences could have been combined. Then prompt to continue.

38. After finishing the first half of the problems, have students switch roles and repeat the procedure.

39. When the students are finished, praise the effort.

40. Say, "Today we worked on combining sentences by using words that can connect two short sentences. These words made the sentences you wrote easier to understand and more interesting."

41. Say, "Remember, I want you to try to use this trick you have learned to combine sentences in your regular classroom or anywhere else when you are not with me. You can use the trick when you are talking or when you are writing sentences. Tomorrow I will ask you what you used the trick for."

42. Say, "Next lesson we will work with some different and longer sentences."

## LESSON 3

**Materials:** Warm-up sentences (Figure 10.11), sheet with reminder words (*and, but, because*) (Figure 10.12), paragraph-revising practice example (Figure 10.13), and paragraph-revising exercise (Figure 10.14).

**Purpose:** Reviewing concept of sentence combining; connecting sentences with *and, but, because* in open exercises; and revising a paragraph.

### Introduction

1. Say, "Today we are going to spend some time again playing with sentences. We are also going to use what we know about combining sentences to change or revise a paragraph. Before we begin, did you have a chance to use this trick for any sentences you wrote? Tell me about it." Prompt students for responses. Then say, "Remember, try to use the trick when you write. It will help you become a better writer."

### Warm-Up

2. Say, "Let's begin with our warm-ups. We will do the warm-ups out loud. Then we will revise a paragraph by using what we have learned during these past few lessons."

3. Say, "There are all kinds of ways good writers combine sentences. Does anyone remember how we combined the sentences the last lesson? What words did we use?" Elicit responses. Then say, "Today we will continue to learn how to combine sentences with words you can use to stick two short sentences together. These words will help you write your sentences in different ways and will help make your sentences more interesting."

4. Set out the warm-up sentence sheet for this lesson (Figure 10.11) and the sheet with the reminder words (Figure 10.12). Cover all but the first set of sentences on the warm-up sheet. Ask for a volunteer to read the sentences aloud. Then explain, "Today you will not have a word behind each sentence cluster to help you put the two short sentences together. You can use the three words we have used, or you can combine the sentences in another way. Here are the words that we have used so far." Ask for ideas on how to put the sentences together. Praise the effort.

5. Write down one example from each student for each pair of sentences.

6. Finish the warm-up sentences.

1. Tom showed the worm to Billy.
   Billy did not want to see the worm.

2. Billy made a face when he saw the worm.
   The worm was brown and slimy.

3. Tom put the worm on a plate.
   Tom gave the plate to Billy.

4. Billy said he would eat the worm.
   Billy wanted ketchup to put on the worm.

**FIGURE 10.11.** Lesson 3 warm-up sentences. (The sentences here and in Figure 10.14 are again from *How to Eat Fried Worms* by Thomas Rockwell, 1973.)

7. Ask the students, "How are we able to do what we've been doing? How did we know how to put the sentences together?" Prompt them to say that we do it by:

   a. Using connecting words (words that help fit two sentences together).

   b. Getting rid of words we don't need.

   c. Moving words around.

   d. Changing some words (word endings).

   e. Adding words if we want to.

8. Show them where they did some of these different operations in the sentences they wrote.

**Revising Practice**

9. Say, "You have been practicing with two simple sentences at a time. Today you will practice with many simple sentences. You will combine the sentences into a more interesting paragraph. Let me show you an example." Show and read the example in Figure 10.13.

**And**

**But**

**Because**

**FIGURE 10.12.** Reminder words.

1. Joe had a hat.

2. Sam had a hat.

3. Joe's hat was white.

4. Sam's hat was blue.

5. Jim liked Sam's hat.

6. Sam's hat was blue.

Joe and Sam had hats. Joe's hat was white, but Sam's hat was blue. Jim liked Sam's hat because it was blue.

**FIGURE 10.13.** Lesson 3 paragraph-revising practice example.

10. Then say, "When you write your paragraph, do not leave out any important information when you combine the sentences. Use everything you have learned to help you write the new paragraph. You may add words, change words, delete words, and rearrange words. You may work together to write the paragraph. You should talk with each other to decide on the best way to revise the simple sentences. You will have 8 minutes to finish." Hand students the paragraph-revising exercise (Figure 10.14). Ask, "Are there any questions?" Answer any questions they ask, and then say, "Begin."

11. When the students have finished, ask for a volunteer to read the paragraph. (If the students are not finished, stop them after 8 minutes.) Praise the effort and reinforce the use of SC. Discuss what the volunteer has changed and why. Ask whether they like the new version better and why.

12. Then ask the students to look for two ways they could revise the paragraph to make it different from their first version (by adding, deleting, or moving words). Help them do this if needed.

13. Give them 2 minutes to make the changes. Then have a volunteer read the new paragraph, and ask the students to discuss whether they like this version better and why.

14. Say, "Today we worked on combining sentences with words that can connect two short sentences. These words made the sentences you wrote easier to understand and more interesting. We also revised a paragraph of simple sentences to make it sound better and more interesting."

1.  Tom made a bet with Billy.
2.  Joe made a bet with Billy.

3.  Billy would win $50.
4.  Billy had to eat 15 worms.

5.  Billy had to eat a worm every day.
6.  Billy had to eat every bit of the worm.

7.  Joe thought Billy would quit.
8.  Billy did not want to quit.

9.  Billy wanted to win the bet.
10.  Billy wanted to win the $50.

11.  Joe tried to trick Billy to stop him from eating worms.
12.  Billy figured out Joe's tricks.

13.  Billy ate all the worms.
14.  Billy won the bet.

**FIGURE 10.14.** Lesson 3 paragraph-revising exercise.

15. Say, "Remember, I want you to try to use this trick you have learned to combine sentences in your regular classroom or anywhere else when you are not with me. You can use the trick when you are talking or when you are writing sentences. Tomorrow I will ask you again what you used the trick for."

16. Say, "Tomorrow you are going to write a story and then make it better by using the tricks we have been practicing."

## LESSON 4

**Materials:** Sentence-Combining Quiz (Figure 10.15).

**Purpose:** Assessment of SC learning.

## Introduction

1. Say, "Today you are going to show me what you have learned about combining sentences. Before we begin, did you have a chance to use this trick for combining any sentences you wrote? Tell me about it." Prompt students for responses. Then say, "Remember, try to use the trick when you write. It will help you become a better writer."

## Testing

2. Say, "Yesterday you worked with each other to write a paragraph. Today you will have a chance to show me what you have learned in this unit. You will combine several sentences on your own." Hand students the Sentence-Combining Quiz (Figure 10.15 on p. 96).
3. Say, "Here are the directions. This is a test of what you have learned about combining sentences. Use everything you have learned to help you combine the sentences. This includes putting sentences together, adding, deleting, and moving parts. Read each problem carefully. Then write out the new sentence combination on the blank line. Read over your answer carefully to make sure it is a good thumbs-up sentence. Are there any questions?" Answer any questions they ask, and then say, "You will have 5 minutes to finish, so work quickly. Begin." Time them for 10 minutes. Tell them when they have 2 minutes and then 1 minute to finish.
4. When the students have finished, collect the papers. Praise the effort.

The next chapter includes a wide range of practice activities.

**Directions:** Read each pair of sentences. Use what you have learned to combine the pair into a better sentence. Read your answers to decide whether they are good sentences. Good luck!

1. Billy wanted to use ketchup.

   Billy thought ketchup would make the worm taste better.

   _____

   _____


2. They started to dig under a tree in the apple orchard.

   The ground was too hard to dig.

   _____

   _____


3. They looked under some flat rocks.

   They found a huge night crawler.

   _____

   _____


4. Billy put the worm on a fork.

   Billy poked the fork in his mouth.

   _____

   _____


5. Tom did not believe he ate the worm.

   Tom thought the worm was too big to eat.

   _____

   _____

**FIGURE 10.15.** Sentence-Combining Quiz. (The sentences here are again from *How to Eat Fried Worms* by Thomas Rockwell, 1973.)

CHAPTER 11

# Practice Activities

$S$C exercises can be practiced in many different types of activities. The mantra guiding any practice activity is "fun!" The activities should engage the students through creative ways to *manipulate and discuss* language in an atmosphere of *play and discovery*. They should never be "drill and kill."

Here is one example of a very simple individual practice activity:

- Place a card with kernel sentences to be combined on a table in front of a student. (Solutions for the exercise are written on the reverse side of the card.)
- The student reads the sentences silently and then suggests how they can be combined.
- After providing a solution, the student turns the card over and checks his or her responses by reading the combined sentences aloud.

This chapter presents other fun practice activities.

## A TALE OF TWO COMBINATIONS

Provide a set of kernels and have the students produce two syntactically different versions. Each version should contain sentence formats that have been taught. This type of exercise helps students create versions of discourse and then choose which sounds better.

## TEN DIFFERENT WAYS

Display a sentence cluster to the students and model 10 different ways the kernels could be combined. Then display another set of kernels and challenge students to combine them in at least 10 different ways. Discuss the students' solutions, and display the best solutions on a bulletin board.

## SENTENCE SPREAD-OUT

Play sentence expansion games with the whole class (Moffett, 1968). Through sentence expansion, students can flesh out basic sentences while working with the syntactic structures they are also combining.

- Begin with a base clause, such as *The teacher began with a short sentence*. Then provide lists of details, attributes, and actions:
  o Details: *handsome, friendly, skilled, debonair, demanding*
  o Attributes: *a skilled speaker, a sensitive and dedicated individual, a person whose shoes are untied*
  o Actions: *struggled desperately to get responses, helped the class to write longer sentences*
- From generated ideas, you can demonstrate how information can be packaged in sentences.
- Then provide a new base clause and have students generate lists of ideas for details, attributes, and actions.
- From the ideas generated, have students (by themselves or in pairs) create as many sentences as they can.

## INDEX CARDS

If some of your students have poor handwriting skills, write words on index cards and have students arrange the words into different sentence combinations. This also makes an effective group or individual activity, as it reduces the transcription burden and involves kinesthetics.

## SENTENCE MIX-UP

Another kinesthetic activity can be created by placing phrases and clauses on separate cards and asking volunteers to move the cards around to create grammatically acceptable sentence. For example, you can write each of these phrases on separate cards and challenge students to create as many sentences as possible:

After school          the boys          played football

Students can either write their solutions on paper or discuss them orally. You may want to allow the students to change the words as needed and add punctuation as required.

## NOTE REWRITE

For students in the upper grades, assign the task of rewriting classroom notes for homework (Moffett, 1968). Prompt students to focus on combining the short sentences they often produce during the note-taking process into syntactic combinations they are learning. This will provide practice in combining sentences, while having the students rehearse the content-area material as well.

## THE EDITOR

During the revision process, have the students change one of their own pieces of writing. The goal is for them to find two or three places to add sentence variety, ideally by using the SC skills that have been taught.

## THE PROOFREADER

To increase awareness of the SC skills being practiced, have students proofread each other's work. Have each student identify one sentence that seems to be effectively constructed in a partner's work, and one place where there could be a revision.

## TEAMWORK

Students can also collaboratively revise compositions. During this revising, provide each pair of students with a checklist of SC skills they could use to improve sentences in each of their drafts. Direct the students to circle places in each draft where SC could be effectively used, and ask them also to highlight the sentences they changed in the final copy.

## FANBOYS

One of the most important organizational truths writers must recognize is that clauses must be semantically linked, both within and between sentences, by connectors that help express meaning. Your students will benefit from a reference chart that lists connectors they can use. Therefore, provide students with such a chart, and then have them practice connecting sentences. A basic chart can include the acronym "FANBOYS" (see Figure 11.1). A more comprehensive version is provided in Figure 11.2.

To help students practice expressing meaning through using appropriate connectors, provide sentences with overt connectors. Then have them replace these connective expressions with contradictory types. Some may be funny; some may not make sense; and some may preserve the original intent of the text. Open discussion of the effects of various connectors will help students to understand how to choose effective connectors in their own writing.

To help students mindfully analyze their own writing, ask them to revise the openings of their sentences and paragraphs to make them more varied and interesting. Here are several additional methods to engage students in paragraph practice.

## PARAGRAPH DOCTOR

Have students diagnose paragraph unity and coherence by rewriting particular sentences within paragraphs from different genres of writing—either to achieve a particular rhetorical effect, or just to try to state an idea in a different or better way. The idea is for students to practice exploring different ways to express an idea while

| Connector | Clause 1 | Clause 2 | Complex sentence |
|---|---|---|---|
| **For** (reason) | Kristie couldn't go home. | She had no way to go. | Kristie couldn't go home, *for* she had no way to go. |
| **And** (addition) | Chris took a bus. | Steve drove home. | Chris took a bus, *and* Steve drove home. |
| **Nor** (and not) | Alex didn't want help. | Alex didn't ask for it. | Alex didn't want help, *nor* did he ask for it. |
| **But** (contrast) | Diego wanted to go late. | Lois wanted to go on time. | Diego wanted to go late, *but* Lois wanted to go on time. |
| **Or** (options) | Latoya bought the new car. | Latoya bought the flat-screen TV. | Latoya bought the new car, *or* Latoya bought the flat-screen TV. |
| **Yet** (unexpected outcome) | April bought the new car. | She didn't know how she was going to pay for it. | April bought the new car, *yet* she didn't know how she was going to pay for it. |
| **So** (result) | It was raining. | The baseball game was delayed. | It was raining, *so* the baseball game was delayed. |

**FIGURE 11.1.** FANBOYS mnemonic.

| Broad meaning | Across-sentence connectives | Within-sentence connectives (coordinators and subordinators) |
|---|---|---|
| Addition | also, too, similarly, in addition, even, indeed, let alone, furthermore, further, moreover | and, as, like |
| Sequential position | first, then, and then, thereupon, next, finally, earlier, previously | and, and then, before, after once, when, as soon as |
| Simultaneous state | meanwhile, at the same time, simultaneously | and, as, when, while, during |
| Choice | or, otherwise | or, either, nor, and neither |
| Opposition | however, nevertheless, on the other hand, in contrast, though, alternatively, anyway, yet, in fact, even so | but, or, (al)though, whereas, while |
| Reinforcing | besides, anyway, after all | |
| Explaining | for example, for instance, in other words, that is to say, i.e., e.g., thus | in that, since, as |
| Listing | first(ly), second(ly), . . ., first of all, finally, lastly, for one thing . . . for another, in the first place, to begin with, next, in sum, to conclude, in a nutshell | and |
| Illustration | for example, for instance, to illustrate | such as, like, namely |
| Comparison | likewise, similarly, too | and, just as, more than, as if, as though |
| Indicating result | therefore, consequently, as a result, so, then, hence, thus, accordingly | because, since, as, for, if, unless, now (that), so (that), in case, provided (that), whether . . . or . . . |
| Indicating time | then, meanwhile, later, afterward, before (that), since (then), meanwhile | when, before, after, since, until, till, while, as, once, whenever |

**FIGURE 11.2.** Sentence connectives, coordinators, and subordinators.

coming to the realization that some versions produced will be more effective than others in certain situations, depending on the audience.

## WHERE DOES IT BELONG?

To help students learn to place information logically within a paragraph, have them insert a sentence with a particular SC construction within a prewritten paragraph.

You can designate a place where the sentence should be inserted, or you can provide the content and see where the students might place the new information. Model also how, when the sentence is inserted, they might have to adjust the construction of the sentences around the inserted sentence to improve the flow and rhythm of the paragraph.

## PARAGRAPH CHALLENGE

Provide students with a paragraph. Then challenge the students to change the number of sentences within the paragraph (e.g., to tighten a four-sentence paragraph into a three-, or a five- into a four- or three-). Discussion should center on which of the various solutions are most appropriate for the audience and the rhetorical goals of the assignment.

- You can also ask the students to keep the length of the paragraph relatively constant (in terms of numbers of words) while increasing or decreasing the number of sentences.
- Or you can direct them to increase the length of the paragraph by a given number of words while keeping the number of sentences constant.

## SENTENCE HUNT

Have students select interesting sentences from reading selections that match the type of sentence being practiced. Then create a bulletin board of sentences students have composed that are very similar to the professionally written sentences.

## JOURNALING

Use SC problems as journal starters to prompt students to practice the constructions in their daily personal writing (Strong, 1986). These exercises can be mini-assignments that help structure transition times between other tasks.

The exercises can be created from famous or funny quotations, such as "Early to rise and early to bed make a male healthy, wealthy, and dead." (James Thurber). Here is an example of how this could be decombined into kernels:

> Early to bed makes a male healthy.
> It makes him wealthy.
> It makes him dead.

Or content-area information can be a source. For example:

Washington was famous.
He was our first president. (because)

## WHICH IS BETTER?

Here is a great exercise to demonstrate the effects of sentence variety in terms of length and style. Read aloud a paragraph-length SC exercise in two forms: the first containing only short, uncombined sentences, and the second a series of long, monotonous sentences that follow the same basic pattern. Help the students to see that both versions have readability problems. Then challenge the students to create versions of their own by varying the sentence length and the structure of the sentences. Finally, have students read their versions to each other so they can see how others have altered the sentence length and structure.

All three versions make for a great bulletin board display. Place the versions with the short, choppy sentences on one side and the ones with the long, unvaried sentences on the other. In between the two extremes, place the versions students have created that help emphasize the point behind SC exercises.

## ARTIST STUDY

Study professionally written paragraphs with your students, and determine whether and how sentences can be written in alternative ways. Using books your students are currently reading can also help them rehearse the content.

Start by drawing a selection from good writing—for example, from Victor Hugo's (1862/1992) *Les Misérables*:

> Without being conscious of what she was experiencing, Cosette felt that she was seized by this black enormity of nature. It was not merely terror that held her, but something more terrible even than terror. (p. 329)

Then have the students decombine the passage into kernels. For example:

> Cosette felt seized.
> Her experiences were not conscious. (without)
> The seizure was by an enormity of nature.
> The enormity was black.
> The enormity was not merely terror.
> It was something more terrible even than terror.

Next, direct the students to recombine the kernels into a passage containing two sentences. Then have students compare their versions with the original; some may come in very close to the author's own work. Spend time discussing the similarities and differences between the author's work and that of the students.

## PREWRITING AND PREREADING

Take another selection from good writing—for example, the opening lines of *All Quiet on the Western Front* by Erich Maria Remarque (1929/1982):

> We are at rest five miles behind the front. Yesterday we were relieved, and now our bellies are full of beef and haricot beans. We are satisfied and at peace. Each man has another mess-tin full for the evening; and, what is more, there is a double ration of sausage and bread. That puts a man in fine trim. (p. 1)

Then decombine the passage into kernels. For example:

> We are at rest.
> We are five miles from the front.
> We were relieved.
> The relief came yesterday.
> Our bellies are now full.
> They are full of beef.
> They are full of haricot beans.
> We are satisfied.
> We are at peace.
> Each man has a second full mess-tin.
> He has that tin for the evening.
> There is a double ration of sausage.
> There is a double ration of beef. (what is more)
> That puts a man in fine trim.

Next, direct the students to recombine the kernels into a passage containing as many sentences as they feel are necessary. Then have students compare their versions with the original; again, some may come in very close to the author's own work.

Finally, reveal the original version as a segue into other prereading activities. Time spent discussing the similarities and differences between the author's prose and their own may make students attend more closely to the author's language as they read the piece.

## STORY STARTERS

Planned starters can provide enough information to give students a good beginning for a story that you want the entire class to wrestle with. Provide the class with a story starter such as the following passage:

## The City

1. We set up our equipment.
   We made some measurements.
   The measurements were preliminary.
   We prepared ourselves mentally.

2. The city lay in the valley.
   The city was ravaged.
   The valley was treeless.
   Smoke still rose in columns.

3. We stumbled forward.
   We surveyed the destruction.
   We understood something.
   Our training had been top-secret.

Then direct the students to combine and modify the kernels to fit their own ideas. They may also arrange the transformations in any order that makes sense to them.

After the students have completed their revisions to the opening that you have provided, direct the class to go ahead and add content to complete the story. One of the best elements of this activity is the comparison of the students' eventual products. There are likely to be many interesting solutions for the kernels, and perhaps even more interesting endings for the story!

I begin the next chapter with a list of common grammatical terms. Then I explain the benefits of two instructional approaches: teaching exercises according to a predetermined sequence, or teaching based on students' individual needs.

CHAPTER 12

# Common Grammatical Terms and Exercise Sequence

## A LIST OF COMMON GRAMMATICAL TERMS

This chapter begins with an alphabetical list of common grammatical terms. These terms provide a common vocabulary for discussion purposes and for understanding the objective of each exercise, as well as the exercise sequence presented later in this chapter (see Table 12.1) and in Chapter 13. They need not be taught directly, nor should definitional knowledge of the terms be tested. Instead, students should grow to understand through direct practice how to create sentences by using these structures and parts of speech.

**Absolute phrases.** An absolute phrase consists of a noun plus at least one other word. It can add details about, or describe a feature of, someone or something mentioned in a different place in the sentence.

**Adjectives and adverbs.** Adjectives and adverbs are modifiers that add meaning to other words and represent a basic way of expanding a sentence. Adjectives modify nouns, whereas adverbs modify verbs, adjectives, and other adverbs. Adjectives identify who, which, what kind, or how many; adverbs identify time, place, manner, degree, or reason.

**Adjective clauses.** Subordination allows a writer to make one idea in a sentence less important (or subordinate) to another. An adjective clause can be used to subordinate ideas. An adjective clause usually begins with a word called a "relative pronoun" (e.g., *who, which, that*), which relates the information from the adjective clause to a word or a phrase in the main clause. A relative pronoun modifies a noun. Of the three most common relative pronouns, *who* refers to people, *which* to things, and *that* to things (or sometimes people, although this use is not universally accepted).

**Adverb clauses.** An adverb clause is always dependent on (or subordinate to) an independent clause. An adverb clause usually modifies a verb, although it may also be used to modify an adjective, an adverb, or even the rest of the sentence. An adverb clause begins with a subordinating conjunction (see below).

**Appositives.** An appositive is a word or word group that identifies or renames another word in a sentence—usuall the noun immediately preceding it in the sentence. Appositive constructions provide a succinct method to describe or define persons, places, or things.

**Clauses.** A clause is any group of words containing a subject and a predicate.

**Complements.** A complement is any word or phrase that completes the sense of a subject, an object, or a verb. For example:

The team named Carl the captain to keep him happy.

Here, the noun *captain* complements the noun *Carl*; the adjective *happy* complements the object *him*.

**Complex sentences.** Complex sentences contain an independent and a dependent clause. For example:

Though the men were tired, they would not move.

**Compound sentences.** Compound sentences contain at least two independent clauses, but no dependent clauses. For example:

We spoke with John for 20 minutes, but he would not agree to come.

**Coordinating conjunctions.** Coordinating conjunctions (*for, and, nor, but, or, yet, so*) connect equal structures—two or more nouns, phrases, or clauses. For example:

Bruce and Kristie enjoyed the game.

**Coordination.** Coordination is a common way to connect related words, phrases, and entire clauses. It involves connecting these sentence elements by using a coordinating conjunction (see above).

**Dependent clauses.** A dependent clause has a subject and a predicate, but does not make a complete statement. For example:

What we are seeing . . .
That he can speak . . .

**Extraposition.** Extraposition is the process or result of moving an element from its usual place to a place at or near the end of a sentence.

**Gerunds.** Gerunds are nouns formed from verbs by adding *-ing*.

**Independent clauses.** Independent clauses can stand alone without any other information; they represent complete thoughts. For example:

The fastest boy took over the flag.

**Nominatives.** Nominatives are nouns or other parts of speech that generally mark the subject of a verb or the predicate noun or predicate adjective. For example:

*The boy* ate spaghetti.
*The spaghetti* has been eaten.
*Kennedy* was a *popular president.*

**Participles/participial phrases.** A participle is a verb form that is used as an adjective to modify nouns and pronouns. Participles and participial phrases (phrases that begin with participles) add information to our sentences. Present-tense participles end in *-ing,* and past participles of all regular verbs end in *-ed.* However, irregular verbs can have a variety of past-participle endings.

**Prepositional phrases.** Prepositional phrases add meaning to the nouns and verbs in sentences, in a similar manner to adjectives and adverbs. A prepositional phrase contains two parts: a preposition, and a noun or a pronoun functioning as the object of the preposition.

**Pronominals.** A pronominal either describes something related to a pronoun or is a phrase that acts as a pronoun. For example:

I want *this ball.*
*Eating that* is very fattening.

**Pronouns.** Pronouns take the place of particular nouns.

**Relative clauses.** Relative clauses are subordinate clauses that modify nouns (most commonly) or noun phrases. For example:

The man *who had a gray beard* spoke very slowly.
The dogs *that could jump high enough* made it over the fence.

**Simple sentences.** A simple sentence is simple because it only contains a single subject and one main verb.

**Subordinating conjunctions.** A subordinating conjunction connects unequal structures, such as an independent and a dependent clause. For example:

Although you went to the game, you should have stayed home.

Many subordinating conjunctions can be used to represent a writer's specific intent. See Figure 12.1 for a list.

Although these simplified explanations provide a common vocabulary, which can be valuable during later discussions, students will need to work with and use each of these terms to completely understand their roles and importance in sentence creation. Do not rely on lectures or worksheets to teach these terms; if you do, you are not likely to achieve the results you are hoping for. Instead, use actual writing and discussion. Build sentences slowly from nouns and verbs by adding elements until you push the simple sentences to their maximum limits.

| Place | Cause | Condition | Concession and comparison | Time |
|-------|-------|-----------|---------------------------|------|
| Where | As | Even if | Although | After |
| Wherever | Because | If | As | As soon as |
| | In order that | In case | As though | As long as |
| | Since | Provided that | Even though | Before |
| | So that | Unless | Just as | Once |
| | | | Though | Still |
| | | | Whereas | Till |
| | | | While | Until |
| | | | | When |
| | | | | Whenever |
| | | | | While |

**FIGURE 12.1.** Commonly used subordinating conjunctions.

## EXERCISE SEQUENCE

There are two choices for the order in which you teach SC exercises. You can have your entire class work through a sequence of exercises presented in a systematic sequence, or you can only teach constructions that are lacking in your students' writing.

If you have the class work through a sequence of exercises, students will be exposed to the same constructions at the same time. This will allow you to monitor all students' progress on similar content. Using sequenced exercises also has the advantage of providing a more incremental instructional approach, allowing all students to be exposed to a corpus of syntactic combinations that they can use in their writing.

Unfortunately, research has yet to determine the most effective order for teaching SC skills. However, there are well-thought-out suggestions for sequencing SC skills, based on studies of natural oral and written language development. Table 12.1 lists exercises in a sequence based loosely on guidelines created by Lawlor (1983) and Cooper (1973). (This same sequence is followed in Chapter 13.) The sequence in Table 12.1 is best taught one skill at a time, beginning with the coordinate structures and progressing through the free modifiers as students' comfort with the constructions improve. The rate at which new skills can be introduced will depend on the age of your students, their abilities, and the time available. Keep your students' knowledge of prior learned constructions strong by continuing to practice those skills while introducing new ones.

If you decide to teach only constructions that are lacking in your students' writing, you will need to discover the areas of weakness in your students' writing and then use Table 12.1 to choose appropriate constructions. To do this, analyze students' writing samples to determine what skills need to be acquired. Note, for example, whether the writing contains any of these common problems: (1) an overrepresentation of short, choppy sentences that detract from the enjoyment of the passage; (2) sentences that are only serially connected with *and*; or (3) sentences that begin in the same manner or are all constructed in the same or very similar arrangements.

For example, what obvious problems do you see in the following passage?

### The Beach Is Cool

One reason that the beach is so cool is the ocean. You can surf on the ocean. You can build a sand castle. You can lie on the sand and get a tan from the sun. You can surf on waves and let the breeze go through your hair. You can play in the waves and have them knock you down. You can get hit by them while surfing. You can surf on the waves. It's fun to surf.

This passage lacks sentence variety, as many sentences start the same way. To help students vary their sentences, provide a list of function or connecting words, and have them practice combining the sentences in the paragraph while also varying the first word. Model revising a sample paragraph for them, and then revise an additional paragraph together. Finally, assign the students a paragraph to revise independently, and then have them share their solutions with the class. Resources students can use for help with combining, varying, and otherwise revising their sentences are provided in Figures 12.2 and 12.3.

Here is a second example with a different problem:

One day there were two animals they tried to get across some land but they could not. Why is because the land split into a half so they had no way to get across.

In this passage the author is plagued by hypercomplexity; the thoughts are too jumbled up to be understood. The sentences in this case should be decombined. For example:

One day there were two animals.
They tried to get across some land.
They could not get across. (but)
The land split in half. (because)

The kernels can then be recombined, leading (ideally) to a much clearer version than the original.

**TABLE 12.1. Suggested Sequence of Sentence-Combining Skills**

<u>Coordinate structures</u>

| | |
|---|---|
| Compound sentence (*and*)<br>Compound sentence (*for*)<br>Compound sentence (*nor*)<br>Compound sentence (*yet*)<br>Compound sentence (*so*)<br>Compound sentence (*but*)<br>Compound sentence (*or*) | Judy raked the lawn, and John watered the flowers. |
| Compound structure with predicate phrase | Ellen ordered a *hamburger and a Coke.* |
| Compound subjects | *Susan and Dave* went to the movies. |
| Compound prenominal adjectives | The *cold and hungry* campers huddled around the fire. |
| Compound objects of prepositions and verbals | The train stopped in *large cities and small villages.*<br>She expects to visit *the museum and the cathedral.* |

<u>Adverb structures</u>

| | |
|---|---|
| Single-word adverbs | Jack walked *carefully.* |
| Prepositional phrases of place/motion | Maria hit the ball *over the fence.* |
| Adverb clauses of time | I finished the test *before the bell rang.* |
| Adverb clauses of reason | We stopped for lunch *because we were hungry.* |
| Prepositional phrases of time | Jim visited the zoo *on Saturday.* |
| Adverb clauses of condition | We'll go on a hike *if the rain stops soon.* |
| Adverbial infinitives | Rick is waiting *to hear from you.* |
| Prepositional phrases of cause, manner, and concession | The picnic was canceled *because of bad weather.*<br>The bomb exploded *with a muffled roar.*<br>Jerry learned to skate *despite his disability.* |
| Adverb clauses of concession and purpose | *Although the sun was shining,* the air was very cool.<br>He fixed the door *so that it wouldn't squeak.* |

<u>Noun modifiers</u>

| | |
|---|---|
| Single-word prenominal adjectives: before subject | The *yellow* canary flew out the window. |
| Single-word prenominal adjectives: before object or predicate nominative | I saw a *yellow* canary. |

*(cont.)*

**TABLE 12.1.** *(cont.)*

| | |
|---|---|
| **Noun modifiers** *(cont.)* | |
| Single-word prenominal adjectives: before object of a preposition | He fell from the *steep* roof. |
| Compound adjectives | She dated the *fun-loving* guy. |
| Adjective clause embeddings: *who/ whom, when, which, that,* or *where* | People *who* live in glass houses should not throw stones. These are the days *when* I am discouraged. He heard the group's new song, *which* had a nice beat. Rover was the dog *that* I saw earlier. That was the town *where* we stopped for dinner. |
| Relative clauses modifying object: Relative pronoun as possessive | The doctor treated a man *whose leg was broken.* |
| Relative clauses modifying subject: Relative pronoun as possessive | Kelsey, *whose purse was stolen,* reported the theft to the police. |
| Adjectival prepositional phrases | The girl *on the porch* is my sister. |
| Nonrestrictive appositive phrases | My neighbor, *the race car driver,* took me around the track. |
| Restrictive appositives | My friend *Rita* won the spelling bee. |
| Postnominal participial phrases: present and past | My teacher is the woman *talking to Steve.* We toured a castle *built many years ago.* |
| Prenominal participles: present and past | That *barking* dog kept us awake all night. These cans are made of *recycled* aluminum. |
| Other adjective clusters/phrases | The masked man, *armed and dangerous,* robbed the bank. *Happy to see her friends,* Yvette ran toward them. |
| **Noun substitutes** | |
| *It* extraposition with noun clauses | *It surprised me* that this movie won no Oscars. |
| *It* extraposition with infinitives | *It was hard to find* a shirt to match these slacks. |
| *It* extraposition with gerunds | *It was wonderful going* to the reunion. |
| **Free modifiers** | |
| Participial phrases: *-ing* and *-ed* | Ted stood on the bridge, *staring at the river below.* We ate the food *prepared by the chef.* |
| Absolutes | *Her heart pounding,* Margarita answered the doorbell. |

## Words That Can Help You Combine Sentences

| | | |
|---|---|---|
| after | since | whereas |
| although | than | while |
| as | that | who |
| as if | though | which |
| as long as | till | what |
| as though | until | whose |
| because | unless | where |
| before | when | when |
| if | whenever | why |
| in case | where | how |
| once | wherever | |

## Words for Additional Ideas

| | | |
|---|---|---|
| and | moreover | likewise |
| furthermore | similarly | also |
| who | whose | whom |
| which | that | |

## Words for Contrasting Ideas

| | | |
|---|---|---|
| but | yet | so |
| though | whereas | on the other hand |
| even though | instead | although |
| otherwise | nevertheless | still |
| however | even | on the contrary |

## Words for Causes and Results

| | | |
|---|---|---|
| so | consequently | as a result |
| therefore | because | thus |
| since | for | |

## Words for Time

| | | |
|---|---|---|
| earlier | beforehand | afterward |
| subsequently | now | at once |
| immediately | later | then |
| finally | meanwhile | |
| previously | thereafter | |

## Words for Giving Specific Information

| | |
|---|---|
| in fact | indeed |

## Words for Choices

| | |
|---|---|
| either | or |
| neither | nor |

## Words for Conditions

| | | |
|---|---|---|
| if | as though | provided |
| unless | as if | as long as |

## Words for Purposes

| | | |
|---|---|---|
| to | that | that |
| so | in order | for |

## Words for Places

| |
|---|
| where |
| wherever |

**FIGURE 12.2.** Lists of words students can use in combining and otherwise reworking sentences.

**Location**

| Above | Below | In back of | On top of |
|---|---|---|---|
| Across | Beneath | In front of | Outside |
| Against | Beside | Inside | Over |
| Along | Between | Into | Throughout |
| Among | Beyond | Near | To the right |
| Around | By | Off | Under |
| Behind | Down | Onto | |

**To Show Time**

| While | Third | Yesterday | Next |
|---|---|---|---|
| After | Now | Soon | As soon as |
| At | Until | Later | When |
| Before | Meanwhile | Afterward | Suddenly |
| During | Today | About | |
| First | Tomorrow | Finally | |
| Second | Next week | Then | |

**Comparing**

| Likewise | As | While | In the same way |
|---|---|---|---|
| Like | Also | Similarly | |

**Contrasting**

| But | Still | Although | On the other hand |
|---|---|---|---|
| However | Yet | Otherwise | Even though |

**Emphasizing a Point**

| Again | To repeat | Especially | For this reason |
|---|---|---|---|
| Truly | In fact | To emphasize | |

**Concluding or Summarizing**

| Finally | As a result | To sum up | In conclusion |
|---|---|---|---|
| Lastly | Therefore | All in all | Because |

**Clarifying**

| That is | For instance | In other words | |
|---|---|---|---|

**Adding Information**

| Again | Another | For instance | For example |
|---|---|---|---|
| Also | And | Moreover | Additionally |
| As well | Besides | Along with | Other |
| Next | Finally | In addition | |

**Qualifiers**

| Almost | Usually | Maybe | Probably |
|---|---|---|---|
| Often | Some | Most | In most cases |

**Concessions**

| Even though | I agree that | I cannot argue with | |
|---|---|---|---|
| While it is true that | Admittedly | Granted | |

**FIGURE 12.3.** Lists of transition words.

Two teaching options for hypercomplexity are (1) to show the original passage and ask students to decombine it into kernels and then recombine the kernels; or (2) to decombine a passage yourself and then have students recombine the kernels, either alone or with a peer. In either case, the writers might be provided with usable solutions.

In the next chapter, I provide a suggested scope of common sentence constructions, presented in a roughly developmental sequence.

CHAPTER 13

# Word-, Phrase-,
# and Clause-Length Exercises

In this chapter a scope of common sentence constructions based loosely on those suggested by Lawlor (1983) and Cooper (1973) is provided. The sentence clusters are presented in a roughly developmental sequence; the order is the same as in Table 12.1. Begin with the simpler constructions and build from there. Match constructions to the level of reading you expect your students to attempt. Use the sentences as exemplars, or templates, that can help you create your own exercises from whatever content source you wish to use.

For all of these exercises, you can use general directions similar to these:

> "Combine these short sentences in the best way you see fit. You must use either the word or words in parentheses, or the underlined word or words, in your new combination."

## Coordinate Structures

Compound Sentence with the Connector *and*

1. **To contrast one idea with another:**
   Bill swept the floor.
   Andy painted the walls. (and)
   **Solution:** Bill swept the floor, *and* Andy painted the walls.

2. **To show that one idea results in another:**
   Juan dropped the flashlight.

He tripped over the chair. (and)
**Solution:** Juan dropped the flashlight, *and* he tripped over the chair.

3. **To indicate a chronological sequence:**
She put the pot of water on the stove.
She turned on the burner. (and)
**Solution:** She put the pot of water on the stove, *and* she turned on the burner.

4. **To suggest an element of surprise:**
The disk crashed through the window.
The disk kept spinning. (and)
**Solution:** The disk crashed through the window, *and* it kept spinning.

5. **To suggest that one clause is conditionally dependent on another:**
Carrie drank too many cans of soda.
She found herself gaining weight. (and)
**Solution:** Carrie drank too many cans of soda, *and* she found herself gaining weight.

6. **To have the second clause comment on the first clause:**
Kristie scored an A on the test.
No one was surprised. (and)
**Solution:** Kristie scored an A on the test, *and* no one was surprised.

## Compound Sentence with the Connector *for*

1. Adrian thought he would win the race.
He had been training very hard. (for)
**Solution:** Adrian thought he would win the race, *for* he had been training very hard.

2. Most of the crowd went home.
The band had stopped playing. (for)
**Solution:** Most of the crowd went home, *for* the band had stopped playing.

3. The players were exhausted.
The game was very long. (for)
**Solution:** The players were exhausted, *for* the game was very long.

4. The leaves fell from the tree.
Autumn had begun. (for)
**Solution:** The leaves fell from the tree, *for* autumn had begun.

5. The man could not sleep.
The sound of the lawnmower was oppressive. (for)
**Solution:** The man could not sleep, *for* the sound of the lawnmower was oppressive.

## Compound Sentence with the Connector *nor*

1.  He is not happy.
    He is not smiling. (nor)
    **Solution:** He is not happy, *nor* is he smiling.

2.  That is not what I heard.
    That is not what I believed. (nor)
    **Solution:** That is not what I heard, *nor* is it what I believed.

3.  The house was not comfortable.
    The house was not charming. (nor)
    The house was not convenient. (nor)
    **Solution:** The house was not comfortable, *nor* was it charming, *nor* was it convenient.

4.  She did not want to hear from him again.
    She did not want to see him again. (nor)
    She did not want to talk to him again. (nor)
    **Solution:** She did not want to hear from him, nor did she want to see him, *nor* did she want to talk to him again.

## Compound Sentence with the Connector *yet*

*Yet* is an interesting connector because it can convey several meanings, including "in addition" ("*yet* another source of happiness"), "even" ("*yet* more prohibitive"), "still" ("she is *yet* a candidate"), "eventually" ("they may *yet* play"), and "so soon as now" ("they are not *yet* at home"). *Yet* can also be used as a coordinating conjunction with a meaning resembling "nevertheless" or "but." Interestingly, using *yet* adds a more distinctive and somewhat more formal tone than *but* can offer. *Yet* can also be acceptably used in tandem with the conjunctions *but, or,* and *and*—for example, *but yet, or yet, and yet.*

1.  Jaydan plays soccer.
    His favorite sport is bowling. (yet)
    **Solution:** Jaydan plays soccer, *yet* his favorite sport is bowling.

2.  The tourists complained about the hot sun.
    They visited the beach every day. (yet)
    **Solution:** The tourists complained about the hot sun, *yet* they visited the beach every day.

3.  She was a smart person.
    She was an absent-minded person. (yet)
    **Solution:** She was a smart *yet* absent-minded person.

4. The team fell behind early.
   It may still win. (yet)
   **Solution:** The team fell behind early, *yet* it may still win.

5. The blanket was worn.
   The girl still used it. (yet)
   **Solution:** The blanket was worn, *yet* the girl still used it.

6. Clay led the league in home runs.
   He was only a rookie. (yet)
   **Solution:** Clay led the league in home runs, *yet* he was only a rookie.

## Compound Sentence with the Connector *so*

1. Eveline was hungry.
   She baked a cake. (so)
   **Solution:** Eveline was hungry, *so* she baked a cake.

2. Conner won a prize.
   He ran all the way home from the carnival. (so)
   **Solution:** Conner won a prize, *so* he ran all the way home from the
   carnival.

3. The map depicted the way out of the cave.
   The boys were able to escape. (so)
   **Solution:** The map depicted the way out of the cave, *so* the boys were able to
   escape.

4. The North and South disagreed on many important ideas.
   There was little hope of preventing a war. (so)
   **Solution:** The North and South disagreed on many basic ideas, *so* there was
   little hope of preventing a war.

5. The president appeared to be an honest man.
   The people voted for him. (so)
   **Solution:** The president appeared to be an honest man, *so* the people voted for
   him.

## Compound Sentence with the Connector *but*

*But* can help a writer in several ways, including underscoring information in
the second clause that unexpectedly contrasts with the information in the first
clause ("Everyone loved the new color, *but* a few thought it too bold"). *But* can also
connect two ideas that imply an exception, with the second word becoming the
subject.

1. Ann knew the answer.
   Bo did not know the answer. (but)
   **Solution:** Ann knew the answer, *but* Bo did not.

2. Many of the colonists wanted to resist the British.
   Some of the colonists remained loyal. (but)
   **Solution:** Many of the colonists wanted to resist the British, *but* some of the colonists remained loyal.

3. Twenty men tried to put the ball in the basket.
   Only one made the shot. (but)
   **Solution:** Twenty men tried to put the ball in the basket, *but* only one made the shot.

## Compound Sentence with the Connector *or*

*Or* can help a writer in several ways. For example, *or* can be used to suggest that only one outcome can be realized, while others cannot: "You can stay dry, *or* you can jump in the water." *Or* can also suggest a possible combination of options: "We can eat Chinese food tonight, *or* we could eat Italian." *Or* can refine an initial clause: "Surrender was the best course of action, *or* so most of us believed." *Or* may also be used to restate or "correct" earlier ideas in the sentence: "Men can be wolves in sheep's clothing, *or* so we are told."

1. Coby may like the soup.
   Coby may like the sandwich. (or)
   **Solution:** Coby may like the soup, *or* he may like the sandwich.

2. Flying saucers could be real.
   Flying saucers could be a hoax. (or)
   **Solution:** Flying saucers could be real, *or* they could be a hoax.

3. The Beatles were the greatest band ever.
   So many people believe. (or)
   **Solution:** The Beatles were the greatest band ever, *or* so many people believe.

4. We were supposed to finish practice at 4:00.
   So the coach had told us. (or)
   **Solution:** We were supposed to finish practice at 4:00, *or* so the coach had told us.

## Compound Structure with Predicate Phrase

1. Charles ordered a veggie burger.
   Charles ordered <u>lemonade</u>.
   **Solution:** Charles ordered a veggie burger *and lemonade*.

2. George Washington was the first president.
   George Washington was a <u>general in the army</u>.
   **Solution:** George Washington was the first president *and a general in the army*.

3. Babe Ruth was a great baseball player.
   Babe Ruth was a <u>hero to many children</u>.
   **Solution:** Babe Ruth was a great baseball player *and a hero to many children*.

4. Gettysburg was a fierce battle.
   Gettysburg was <u>the turning point of the Civil War</u>.
   **Solution:** Gettysburg was a fierce battle *and the turning point of the Civil War*.

5. Flies have two wings.
   Flies have <u>many eyes</u>.
   **Solution:** Flies have two wings *and many eyes*.

## Compound Subjects

1. Bananas are fruits.
   <u>Apples</u> are fruits.
   **Solution:** Bananas *and apples* are fruits.

2. Julian went to the cafeteria.
   <u>Tess</u> went to the cafeteria.
   **Solution:** Julian *and Tess* went to the cafeteria.

3. Utah is a Western state.
   <u>New Mexico</u> is a Western state.
   **Solution:** Utah *and New Mexico* are Western states.

4. The Eastern white pine is a slow-growing evergreen.
   <u>The Scots pine</u> is a slow-growing evergreen.
   **Solution:** The Eastern white pine and *the Scots pine* are slow-growing evergreens.

5. The Boers fought the Zulus in Africa.
   <u>The British</u> fought the Zulus in Africa.
   **Solution:** The Boers *and the British* fought the Zulus in Africa.

## Compound Prenominal Adjectives

1. The dog stood outside the house.
   The dog was <u>cold</u>.
   The dog was <u>wet</u>.
   **Solution:** The *cold and wet* dog stood outside the house.

2. The leaves fell from the tree.
   The leaves were <u>beautiful</u>.

The leaves were <u>delicate</u>.
**Solution:** The *beautiful and delicate* leaves fell from the tree.

3.  The chipmunk darted away.
    The chipmunk was <u>tiny</u>.
    The chipmunk was <u>frightened</u>.
    **Solution:** The *tiny and frightened* chipmunk darted away.

4.  The explorer was James Cook.
    The explorer was <u>intrepid</u>.
    The explorer was <u>cunning</u>.
    **Solution:** The *intrepid and cunning* explorer was James Cook.

## Compound Objects of Prepositions and Verbals

1.  He slept in his bed throughout the morning.
    He slept in his bed throughout the <u>afternoon</u>.
    **Solution:** He slept in his bed throughout the morning *and afternoon*.

2.  The dog jumped over the table.
    The dog jumped over the <u>chairs</u>.
    **Solution:** The dog jumped over the table *and chairs*.

3.  She wants to visit the library.
    She wants to visit the <u>cafeteria</u>.
    **Solution:** She wants to visit the library *and the cafeteria*.

4.  Napoleon Bonaparte's army marched through large cities.
    Napoleon Bonaparte's army marched through <u>small villages</u>.
    **Solution:** Napoleon Bonaparte's army marched through large cities *and small villages*.

5.  The bus stopped next to the store.
    The bus stopped next to the <u>diner</u>.
    **Solution:** The bus stopped next to the store *and the diner*.

## Adverb Structures

### Single-Word Adverbs

1.  Keshawn walked home.
    He walked <u>quickly</u>.
    **Solution:** Keshawn *quickly* walked home.

2.  The lightning cracked.
    The crack was <u>loud</u>.
    **Solution:** The lightning cracked *loudly*.

3. The crabs walked on the beach.
   They walked <u>sideways</u>.
   **Solution:** The crabs walked *sideways* on the beach.

4. The waves crashed on the rocks.
   They crashed <u>savagely</u>.
   **Solution:** The waves crashed *savagely* on the rocks.

5. I have soup for dinner.
   I have soup <u>often</u>.
   **Solution:** I *often* have soup for dinner.

## Prepositional Phrases of Place/Motion

1. Travis hit the ball.
   The ball went <u>over the fence</u>.
   **Solution:** Travis hit the ball *over the fence*.

2. Keely was sitting.
   Keely was <u>on top of the rug</u>.
   **Solution:** Keely was sitting *on top of the rug*.

3. We were crowded together.
   We were <u>in the elevator</u>.
   **Solution:** We were crowded together *in the elevator*.

4. The squirrel ran.
   It ran <u>into the hole</u>.
   **Solution:** The squirrel ran *into the hole*.

5. The words were printed in ink.
   The words were <u>on the bottom of the cup</u>.
   **Solution:** The words were printed in ink *on the bottom of the cup*.

## Adverb Clauses of Time

1. I rang the bell.
   I rang it <u>as soon as I entered the room</u>.
   **Solution:** I rang the bell *as soon as I entered the room*.

2. The Vikings began to attack England.
   The attacks were <u>after they built their long boats</u>.
   **Solution:** The Vikings began to attack England *after they built their long boats*.

3. Amino acids are used to synthesize proteins.
   They synthesize proteins <u>when they are taken into the body</u>.
   **Solution:** Amino acids are used to synthesize proteins *when they are taken into the body*.

4.  Natalya had stopped running.
    The coach blew the whistle. (by the time)
    **Solution:** Natalya had stopped running *by the time the coach blew the whistle.*

5.  The band continued to play.
    The ship was sinking. (while)
    **Solution:** The band continued to play *while the ship was sinking.*

## Adverb Clauses of Reason

1.  We ran away from the house.
    We were frightened. (because)
    **Solution:** We ran away from the house *because we were frightened.*

2.  Gavin cleaned the desks.
    Gavin likes his teacher. (because)
    **Solution:** *Because he likes his teacher,* Gavin cleaned the desks.

3.  Krista was glad.
    Saige joined the team. (that)
    **Solution:** Krista was glad *that Saige joined the team.*

4.  Leonidas commanded respect.
    He was a fierce warrior. (because)
    **Solution:** Leonidas commanded respect *because he was a fierce warrior.*

5.  Aiden quit the team.
    He was most unhappy. (as)
    **Solution:** *As he was most unhappy,* Aiden quit the team.

## Prepositional Phrases of Time

1.  The snow fell heavily.
    It fell before the game.
    **Solution:** The snow fell heavily *before the game.*

2.  He is going to start his diet.
    He will start in January.
    **Solution:** He is going to start his diet *in January.*

3.  She can sit here.
    She can sit until 5:00.
    **Solution:** She can sit here *until 5:00.*

4.  The package may come.
    It may come tomorrow. (as soon as)
    **Solution:** The package may come *as soon as tomorrow.*

5. Jocelyn found $10.
   She found it during her vacation.
   **Solution:** Jocelyn found $10 *during her vacation.*

## Adverb Clauses of Condition

1. I will eat it.
   It tastes good. (if)
   **Solution:** *If* it tastes good, *I will eat it.*

2. I feel woozy.
   I see her. (whenever)
   **Solution:** I feel woozy *whenever I see her.*

3. Many batters will strike out.
   The pitcher is good. (if)
   **Solution:** Many batters will strike out *if the pitcher is good.*

4. Evan will buy a new car.
   Evan wins the lottery. (when)
   **Solution:** *When* Evan wins the lottery, *he will buy a new car.*

5. Weeds grow.
   They put down roots. (whenever)
   **Solution:** Weeds grow *whenever they put down roots.*

## Adverbial Infinitives

1. George is waiting.
   He wants to see you.
   **Solution:** George is waiting *to see you.*

2. Chase studies hard.
   He wants to get good grades.
   **Solution:** Chase studies hard *to get good grades.*

3. Natalie sings songs.
   Natalie wants to entertain people.
   **Solution:** Natalie sings songs *to entertain people.*

4. Gianna went to medical school.
   She is learning anatomy. (to)
   **Solution:** Gianna went to medical school *to learn anatomy.*

5. The teachers assign homework.
   The homework helps students learn. (to)
   **Solution:** The teachers assign homework *to help students learn.*

## Prepositional Phrases of Cause, Manner, and Concession

1. The game was canceled.
   Rain was the cause. (because)
   **Solution:** The game was canceled *because of rain.*

2. The engine started.
   It made a loud roar. (with)
   **Solution:** The engine started *with a loud roar.*

3. Janice was happy.
   She was happy after what had happened. (despite)
   **Solution:** Janice was happy *despite what had happened.*

4. The book was returned.
   It was overdue. (because)
   **Solution:** The book was returned *because it was overdue.*

5. The player swung the bat.
   He swung with great force.
   **Solution:** The player swung the bat *with great force.*

## Adverb Clauses of Concession and Purpose

1. The day was rainy.
   The game was still played. (although)
   **Solution:** *Although* the day was rainy, *the game still was played.*

2. He wanted to eat the soup.
   He did not know what it contained. (even if)
   **Solution:** He wanted to eat the soup, *even if he did not know what it contained.*

3. He is tall.
   He could not reach the box. (although)
   **Solution:** *Although* he is tall, *he could not reach the box.*

4. He rang the doorbell.
   He checked if she was home. (in order to)
   **Solution:** He rang the doorbell *in order to check if she was home.*

5. You must eat well tonight.
   You can run hard tomorrow. (so that)
   **Solution:** You must eat well tonight, *so that you can run hard tomorrow.*

# Noun Modifiers

## Single-Word Prenominal Adjectives: Before Subject

1.  The woodpecker attacked my house.
    The woodpecker was <u>black</u>.
    **Solution:** The *black* woodpecker attacked my house.

2.  The sky has few clouds.
    The sky is <u>hazy</u>.
    **Solution:** The *hazy* sky has few clouds.

3.  The girl came home.
    The girl was <u>beautiful</u>.
    **Solution:** The *beautiful* girl came home.

4.  The host threw a party.
    The host was <u>gracious</u>.
    **Solution:** The *gracious* host threw a party.

5.  The railroad opened in 1869.
    The railroad was the *<u>Pacific</u>*.
    **Solution:** The *Pacific* railroad opened in 1869.

## Single-Word Prenominal Adjectives: Before Object or Predicate Nominative

1.  She ate the pie.
    She ate it <u>whole</u>.
    **Solution:** She ate the *whole* pie.

2.  She has luck.
    Her luck is <u>best</u>.
    **Solution:** She has the *best* luck.

3.  Frederick was a man.
    He was <u>cultured</u>.
    **Solution:** Frederick was a *cultured* man.

4.  Ronald Reagan was an actor.
    He acted <u>formerly</u>.
    **Solution:** Ronald Reagan was a *former* actor.

5.  He attempted the at-bats.
    They were the <u>fewest</u>.
    **Solution:** He attempted the *fewest* at-bats.

## Single-Word Prenominal Adjectives: Before Object of a Preposition

1.  Adam fell.
    He was on the tall ladder. (from)
    **Solution:** Adam fell *from the tall ladder.*

2.  Calculus is a hard subject.
    Many smart students find it hard. (for)
    **Solution:** Calculus is a hard subject *for many smart students.*

3.  The European Union is made up of countries.
    Many countries are in the European Union.
    **Solution:** The European Union is made up of *many* countries.

4.  John pushed the button on the panel.
    The panel was large.
    **Solution:** John pushed the button on the *large* panel.

5.  Kael dove into the waters.
    The waters swirled.
    **Solution:** Kael dove into the *swirling* waters.

## Compound Adjectives

1.  Cooper talked with the girl.
    The girl had brown eyes.
    **Solution:** Cooper talked with the *brown-eyed* girl.

2.  Morgan gave a presentation.
    The presentation lasted 15 minutes.
    **Solution:** Morgan gave a *15-minute* presentation.

3.  Bruno had a mark on his arm.
    The mark was black and blue.
    **Solution:** Bruno had a *black-and-blue* mark on his arm.

4.  The boys sat at the table.
    The table was 10 feet long.
    **Solution:** The boys sat at the *10-foot-long* table.

5.  Blake took his clothes to the Laundromat.
    The Laundromat was self-service.
    **Solution:** Blake took his clothes to the *self-service* Laundromat.

## Adjective Clause Embeddings: *who/whom*

1. The boys stared at Eddie.
   Eddie had jumped straight up in the air. (who)
   **Solution:** The boys stared at Eddie, *who had jumped straight up in the air.*

2. The girls are acting in the play.
   The girls are on the stage. (who)
   **Solution:** The girls *who are on the stage* are acting in the play.

3. The boy appeared to know the answer.
   I asked the boy. (whom)
   **Solution:** The boy *whom I asked* appeared to know the answer.

4. The students passed the test.
   The students studied hard. (who)
   **Solution:** The students *who studied hard* passed the test.

5. Mr. Huang has retired.
   He is a well-respected lawyer. (who)
   **Solution:** Mr. Huang, *who is a well-respected lawyer,* has retired.

## Adjective Clause Embeddings: *when*

1. 1905 was the year.
   The rebellion began then. (when)
   **Solution:** 1905 was the year *when the rebellion began.*

2. The team should not be disturbed.
   The team is practicing. (when)
   **Solution:** The team should not be disturbed *when it is practicing.*

3. This is the inning.
   Our team must score. (when)
   **Solution:** This is the inning *when our team must score.*

4. He was alone on the island.
   He awoke. (when)
   **Solution:** *When he awoke,* he was alone on the island.

5. Please close the door.
   Close it when the bell rings.
   **Solution:** Please close the door *when the bell rings.*

## Adjective Clause Embeddings: *which*

1. Niko is working on the painting.
   The painting must be finished today. (which)
   **Solution:** The painting, which Niko is working on, must be finished today.

2. This book is about the Alamo.
   I bought it yesterday. (which)
   **Solution:** This book, which I bought yesterday, is about the Alamo.

3. Dajuan's cat is driving me crazy.
   The cat lives upstairs. (which)
   **Solution:** Dajuan's cat, *which lives upstairs,* is driving me crazy.

4. The toy boat was never recovered.
   The toy boat sank in the pond. (which)
   **Solution:** The toy boat, *which sank in the pond,* was never recovered.

5. Claire has a dog named Homer.
   The dog follows her everywhere. (which)
   **Solution:** Claire has a dog named Homer, *which follows her everywhere.*

## Adjective Clause Embeddings: *that*

1. The man was wearing a red hat.
   The man saw the plane go by. (that)
   **Solution:** The man *that saw the plane go by* was wearing a red hat.

2. The book report is due Friday.
   Josh is working on the report. (that)
   **Solution:** The book report *that Josh is working on* is due Friday.

3. These are the books.
   I need the books for the project. (that)
   **Solution:** These are the books *that I need for the project.*

4. He is a type of person.
   You can trust him. (that)
   **Solution:** He is the type of person *that you can trust.*

5. It was the biggest pumpkin.
   You could imagine. (that)
   **Solution:** It was the biggest pumpkin *that you could imagine.*

## Adjective Clause Embeddings: *where*

1. The house is called Mount Vernon.
   George Washington lived in the house. (where)
   **Solution:** The house *where George Washington lived* is called Mount Vernon.

2. The field is 2 miles away.
   We practiced at the field. (where).
   **Solution:** The field *where we practiced* is 2 miles away.

3. That's the mountain.
   The bear was found. (where)
   **Solution:** That's the mountain *where the bear was found.*

4. The building is old and dilapidated.
   They work in the building. (where)
   **Solution:** The building *where they work* is old and dilapidated.

5. The room was locked.
   We stored the toys in the room. (where)
   **Solution:** The room *where we stored the toys* was locked.

## Relative Clauses Modifying Object: Relative Pronoun as Possessive

1. We met a woman.
   Her son is a musician. (whose)
   **Solution:** We met a woman *whose son is a musician.*

2. I know the student.
   The student's test was lost. (whose)
   **Solution:** I know the student *whose test was lost.*

3. I see the man.
   His car was washed. (whose)
   **Solution:** I see the man *whose car was washed.*

4. Maren was the girl.
   We coveted her purse. (whose)
   **Solution:** Maren was the girl *whose purse we coveted.*

5. Jordan was the player.
   We needed his help the most. (whose)
   **Solution:** Jordan was the player *whose help we needed the most.*

## Relative Clauses Modifying Subject: Relative Pronoun as Possessive

1. Dr. Asaro will be the speaker.
   Her dissertation was just published. (whose)
   **Solution:** Dr. Asaro, *whose dissertation was just published,* will be the speaker.

2. The young man walked into the room.
   I could not recall his name. (whose)
   **Solution:** The young man, *whose name I could not recall,* walked into the room.

3. The car was wet inside after the rain.
   The window was open. (whose)
   **Solution:** The car, *whose window was open,* was wet inside after the rain.

4. Jack came to the meeting.
   His son was a famous ballplayer.
   **Solution:** Jack, *whose son was a famous ballplayer,* came to the meeting.

5. José painted the room alone.
   His brother had a broken hand. (whose)
   **Solution:** José, *whose brother had a broken hand,* painted the room alone.

## Adjectival Prepositional Phrases

1. The girl is my friend.
   The girl is on the swing.
   **Solution:** The girl *on the swing* is my friend.

2. Robert's work covered many different ideas.
   Robert worked on the planning commission.
   **Solution:** Robert's work *on the planning commission* covered many different ideas.

3. Those three-level houses were built recently.
   The houses are on the south side of town.
   **Solution:** Those three-level houses *on the south side of town* were built recently.

4. The woman is the teacher.
   The woman is in the next room.
   **Solution:** The woman *in the next room* is the teacher.

5. The bridge needs many repairs.
   The bridge is over the river.
   **Solution:** The bridge *over the river* needs many repairs.

## Nonrestrictive Appositive Phrases

1. My neighbor sold me the shoes.
   My neighbor is a salesman.
   **Solution:** My neighbor, *the salesman,* sold me the shoes.

2. James taught all the kids how to serve and volley.
   He is a very good tennis player.
   **Solution:** *A very good tennis player,* James taught all the kids how to serve and volley.

3. The animal is crawling up the oak tree.
   The animal is a squirrel.
   **Solution:** The animal, *a squirrel,* is crawling up the oak tree.

4. My teacher is very nice.
   My teacher is Miss Othmar.
   **Solution:** My teacher, *Miss Othmar,* is very nice.

5. The boys climbed the peak.
   The peak is <u>one of the steepest in the East</u>.
   **Solution:** The boys climbed the peak, *one of the steepest in the East.*

## Restrictive Appositives

1. One of my friends is Sam.
   Sam <u>won the race</u>.
   **Solution:** My friend Sam *won the race.*

2. Bruce asked Kristie whether she had read the novel.
   The novel was *<u>War and Peace</u>*.
   **Solution:** Bruce asked Kristie whether she had read the novel *War and Peace.*

3. One of our coaches yelled at the umpire.
   <u>Manny</u> was the coach.
   **Solution:** Our coach *Manny* yelled at the umpire.

4. One of our neighbors was named vice-president.
   The neighbor is <u>Bob</u>.
   **Solution:** Our neighbor *Bob* was named vice-president.

5. One of Steve's brothers became a baseball player after quitting football.
   <u>Hank</u> is the brother.
   **Solution:** Steve's brother *Hank* became a baseball player after quitting football.

## Postnominal Participial Phrases: Present and Past

1. My brother is the man.
   He is <u>talking to Luke</u>.
   **Solution:** My brother is the man *talking to Luke.*

2. We found a book.
   The book was <u>written many years ago</u>.
   **Solution:** We found a book *written many years ago.*

3. Edwina stared at the dirty dishes.
   The dishes were <u>stacked in the sink</u>.
   **Solution:** Edwina stared at the dirty dishes *stacked in the sink.*

4. We drove a car.
   The car was <u>built in the 1940s</u>.
   **Solution:** We drove a car *built in the 1940s.*

5. We are eating cake.
   The cake is <u>made from scratch</u>.
   **Solution:** We are eating cake *made from scratch.*

## Prenominal Participles: Present and Past

1. That bird woke us up in the morning.
   The bird was <u>squawking</u>.
   **Solution:** That *squawking* bird woke us up in the morning.

2. This bottle is made of plastic.
   The plastic is <u>recycled</u>.
   **Solution:** This bottle is made of *recycled* plastic.

3. They made a fire with wood.
   The wood was <u>seasoned</u>.
   **Solution:** They made a fire with the *seasoned* wood.

4. The cry was heard throughout the store.
   The cry was <u>bellowing</u>.
   **Solution:** The *bellowing* cry was heard throughout the store.

5. The girl had a sore nose.
   The girl was <u>crying</u>.
   **Solution:** The *crying* girl had a sore nose.

## Other Adjective Clusters/Phrases

1. The dog refused to walk.
   The dog was <u>hungry</u>.
   The dog was <u>tired</u>.
   **Solution:** The dog, *hungry and tired,* refused to walk.

2. Anthony finally asked for directions.
   He was <u>unable to find his way home</u>.
   **Solution:** *Unable to find his way home,* Anthony finally asked for directions.

3. When she saw the pilot she felt safer.
   The pilot was <u>so handsome</u>.
   The pilot was <u>so tall</u>.
   **Solution:** When she saw the pilot, *so handsome and tall,* she felt safer.

4. The batter threw his bat away.
   He was <u>angry over the umpire's call</u>.
   **Solution:** *Angry over the umpire's call,* the batter threw his bat away.

5. The man drove to his friend's house.
   The man <u>was lonesome</u>.

The man <u>was sad.</u>
**Solution:** The man, *lonesome and sad,* drove to his friend's house.

# Noun Substitutes

## *It* Extraposition with Noun Clauses

1. My friend came to my house.
   It pleased me.
   **Solution:** It pleased me that my friend came to my house.

2. My neighbor played loud music all night.
   I was bothered.
   **Solution:** It bothered me that my neighbor played loud music all night.

3. Terence was a gifted musician.
   It surprised me.
   **Solution:** It surprised me that Terence was a gifted musician.

4. You remembered me on my birthday.
   It delighted me.
   **Solution:** It delighted me that you remembered me on my birthday.

5. The shirt fit Teri perfectly.
   It made Teri feel good.
   **Solution:** It made Teri feel good that the shirt fit her perfectly.

## *It* Extraposition with Infinitives

1. It took a long time.
   We found the treasure.
   **Solution:** It took a long time to find the treasure.

2. Shannon completed the math homework.
   It was difficult.
   **Solution:** It was difficult for Shannon to complete the math homework.

3. The bear was huge.
   It was frightening.
   **Solution:** It was frightening that the bear was so huge.

4. Miranda flosses her teeth every day.
   It is important.
   **Solution:** It is important that Miranda floss her teeth every day.

5. The food arrived at our table.
   The food was cold.
   It was disappointing.
   **Solution:** It was disappointing that the food arrived at our table cold.

## *It* Extraposition with Gerunds

1. I waited in the car.
   It was boring.
   **Solution:** It was boring waiting in the car.

2. I received a flu shot.
   It hurt.
   **Solution:** It hurt receiving a flu shot.

3. It was exciting.
   I saw my old roommate.
   **Solution:** It was exciting seeing my old roommate.

4. We watched a horror movie
   It was on Channel 7.
   It was scary.
   **Solution:** It was scary watching the horror movie on Channel 7.

5. She drank the ice-cold water.
   It was refreshing.
   **Solution:** It was refreshing drinking the ice-cold water.

# Free Modifiers

## Participial Phrases: *-ing*

1. The students left for the rally.
   They were wearing their school spirit shirts.
   **Solution:** The students left for the rally, wearing their school spirit shirts.

2. The dogs ran down the street.
   The dogs were barking at the mailman.
   **Solution:** The dogs ran down the street, barking at the mailman.

3. The new comedy is coming out next weekend.
   It features Will Smith.
   **Solution:** The new comedy, featuring Will Smith, comes out next weekend.

4. Sam was standing on the roof top.
   He watched the sun rise.
   **Solution:** Standing on the rooftop, Sam watched the sun rise.

5. Austin was walking to the library.
   He witnessed an accident.
   **Solution:** Walking to the library, Austin witnessed an accident.

## Participial Phrases: -*ed*

1. We ate the casserole.
   It was cooked by my father.
   **Solution:** We ate the casserole cooked by my father.

2. We joined the new bowling team.
   It was established by my math teacher.
   **Solution:** We joined the new bowling team, established by my math teacher.

3. My uncle hung the artwork on the fridge.
   It was painted by my cousin.
   **Solution:** My uncle hung the artwork, painted by my cousin, on the fridge.

4. The ladies' room had a long line.
   It was located at the entrance of the park.
   **Solution:** The ladies' room, located at the entrance of the park, had a long line.

5. My sister finally quit her job.
   She was discouraged by the long hours and low pay.
   **Solution:** Discouraged by the long hours and low pay, my sister finally quit her job.

## Absolutes

1. Dominic walked gingerly across the room
   The pain shot through his leg.
   **Solution:** Dominic walked gingerly across the room, pain shooting through his leg.

2. Marley dreamed of a hot cup of cocoa.
   His fingers were frostbitten.
   **Solution:** Marley, his fingers frostbitten, dreamed of a hot cup of cocoa.

3. Alexis ran up the stairs.
   Her heart was racing.
   **Solution:** Alexis ran up the stairs, her heart racing.

4. The movie started already.
   We found a seat.
   **Solution:** The movie having started already, we found a seat.

5. She stood to begin the eulogy.
   Her eyes were welling with tears.
   **Solution:** She stood, eyes welling with tears, to begin the eulogy.

## Using Adjective Phrases (Many Possible Solutions)

**Directions:** "Combine the following pairs of sentences into one sentence with an adjective phrase."

1. Jill did not know what to order.
   She had never eaten in an Indian restaurant.
   **Possible Solutions:**
   Jill, having never eaten in an Indian restaurant, did not know what to order.
   Never having eaten in an Indian restaurant, Jill did not know what to order.

2. The teacher was lost in thought.
   She did not notice that pencils were falling from her bag.
   **Possible Solutions:**
   The teacher, lost in thought, did not notice that pencils were falling from her bag.
   Lost in thought, the teacher did not notice that pencils were falling from her bag.

3. Caleb refused to give up.
   He was committed to a comeback victory.
   **Possible Solutions:**
   Caleb, committed to a comeback victory, refused to give up.
   Committed to a comeback victory, Caleb refused to give up.

4. Ali continued to walk to the bus stop.
   Ali was unconscious of the cold.
   **Possible Solutions:**
   Ali, unconscious of the cold, continued to walk to the bus stop.
   Unconscious of the cold, Ali continued to walk to the bus stop.

5. We ate a dinner.
   Sue prepared the meal.
   Devyn planned the meal.
   **Possible Solutions:**
   We ate a dinner prepared by Sue and planned by Devyn.
   Sue prepared and Devyn planned the dinner we ate.

6. Antony was a great general.
   He was intensely loved by his soldiers.
   He was feared by his enemies.
   **Possible Solutions:**
   Antony, intensely loved by his soldiers and feared by his enemies, was a great general.
   Intensely loved by his soldiers and feared by his enemies, Antony was a great general.

## Using Participial Phrases (Many Possible Solutions)

1.  The professor did not allow enough time for completion.
    He underestimated how hard the book would be to write.
    **Possible Solutions:**
    Underestimating how hard the book would be to write, the professor did not
        allow enough time for completion.
    The professor, underestimating how hard the book would be to write, did not
        allow enough time for completion.

2.  The truck was driven by Karly.
    The truck was carrying the props for the play.
    **Possible Solutions:**
    The truck carrying the props for the play was driven by Karly.
    The truck driven by Karly was carrying the props for the play.

3.  The first baseman ran off the field.
    He thought the inning was over.
    **Possible Solutions:**
    The first baseman, thinking the inning was over, ran off the field.
    Thinking the inning was over, the first baseman ran off the field.

4.  Alisa saw her girlfriends.
    They were walking into a store.
    The store sold clothing.
    **Possible Solutions:**
    Alisa saw her girlfriends walking into the clothing store.

5.  At the north end of the building was the cafeteria.
    The cafeteria smelled of fried fish.
    **Possible Solutions:**
    At the north end of the building was the cafeteria, smelling of fried fish.
    At the north end of the building, smelling of fried fish, was the cafeteria.

## Using Adverbial Clauses (Many Possible Solutions)

1.  The pitcher threw to first base.
    They feared a stolen base. (because)
    **Possible Solutions:**
    Because they feared a stolen base, the pitcher threw to first base.
    The pitcher threw to first base because they feared a stolen base.

2.  The plan succeeded.
    The runner was picked off. (as)
    He was trying to steal second base.
    **Possible Solutions:**
    The plan succeeded, as the runner was picked off trying to steal second base.

3. Ray raised his hand.
   In reality he did not know the answer. (although)
   **Possible Solutions:**
   Ray raised his hand, although in reality he did not know the answer.
   Although in reality he did not know the answer, Ray raised his hand.

4. The team can win many games.
   It will win, provided the players score enough points.
   **Possible Solutions:**
   The team can win many games provided the players score enough points.
   The team can, provided the players score enough points, win many games.

5. Mariah worked.
   She worked as a student should.
   The student is dedicated.
   **Possible Solutions:** Mariah worked as a dedicated student should.

6. We studied for the test.
   Our grades depended on it. (as though)
   **Possible Solutions:** We studied for the test as though our grades depended on
   it.

7. The batter swung.
   He saw the pitch he wanted. (when)
   **Possible Solutions:** When the batter saw the pitch he wanted, he swung.

## Using Adverbial Phrases (Many Possible Solutions)

1. He was selected to be the running back.
   He had speed. (because)
   **Possible Solutions:**
   Because of his speed, he was selected to be the running back.
   He was selected to be the running back because of his speed.

2. The waiter waited patiently.
   Joey was indecisive. (in spite of)
   **Possible Solutions:**
   In spite of Joey's indecision, the waiter waited patiently.
   The waiter waited patiently, in spite of Joey's indecision.

3. Vanessa still wanted the new purse.
   She was happy. (though)
   **Possible Solutions:**
   Though happy, Vanessa still wanted the new purse.

4. The team was going to lose.
   This was according to the sports writer.

**Possible Solutions:**
According to the sports writer, the team was going to lose.
The team was going to lose, according to the sports writer.

5. Caroline had a reputation as a spender.
   This was contrary to the best advice.
   **Possible Solutions:**
   Contrary to the best advice, Caroline had a reputation as a spender.
   Caroline had a reputation as a spender, contrary to the best advice

6. The game went on.
   There was a torrential downpour of rain. (despite)
   **Possible Solutions:**
   The game went on, despite the torrential downpour of rain.
   Despite the torrential downpour of rain, the game went on.

7. I felt much better.
   I spent a day in the mountains. (after)
   **Possible Solutions:**
   After spending a day in the mountains, I felt much better.
   I felt much better after spending a day in the mountains.

   In the next chapter, more complex and challenging exercises are presented.

# CHAPTER 14

# Exercises with Multiple Grammatical Elements

This chapter presents problems that challenge students to create combinations using several different grammatical elements. You can certainly encourage students to add more details/ideas to the combinations, but they should always ensure that the important information is included in each solution. Introduce these exercises to your students by using the directions provided below for each particular type of construction.

## Sentence Construction with Adjectives and Adverbs

**Directions:** "Combine the sentences in each set into a single clear and interesting sentence containing at least one adjective or adverb (or both). Omit needlessly repeated words, but don't take out important details."

1. Grace had long hair and a round face.
   The hair was black.
   The hair was straight.
   The face was freckled.
   **Possible Solution:** Grace had long, straight, black hair and a freckled, round face.

2. The coach threw the player the ball.
   The coach was angry.
   The throw was quick.

The player was startled.

The ball was scuffed.

**Possible Solution:** The angry coach quickly threw the scuffed ball at the startled player.

3.  The TV was plugged in.

    The TV was high-definition.

    The plugging was careful.

    **Possible Solution:** The high-definition TV was carefully plugged in.

4.  The airplane landed.

    The airplane was silver.

    The airplane was large.

    The landing was safe.

    **Possible Solution:** The large silver airplane landed safely.

## Sentence Construction with Prepositional Phrases

**Directions:** "Prepositions show the relation of one word to another word within a sentence. A preposition requires an object to complete it, typically a noun or a pronoun. A prepositional phrase consists of a preposition and its object. Combine the sentences in each set into a single clear sentence containing at least one prepositional phrase. Omit needlessly repeated words, but don't take out important details."

1.  The squirrel darted.

    It darted across the deck.

    This happened in the morning.

    **Possible Solution:** The squirrel darted across the deck in the morning.

2.  Uncle Matt played his guitar.

    He played in the club.

    He played after the dinner.

    The dinner was with Aunt Sue.

    **Possible Solution:** After dinner with Aunt Sue, Uncle Matt played his guitar in the club.

3.  The player dashed, dove, and jumped.

    He dashed down the line.

    He dove to the base.

    He jumped to his feet.

    **Possible Solution:** The player dashed down the line, dove to the base, and jumped to his feet.

4.  Emma played.

    She played with her brother.

She played with their dog.
They played on the porch.
They played in the afternoon.
**Possible Solution:** Emma and her brother played on the porch with their dog in the afternoon.

5. The band played.
   It played on the field.
   It played during the halftime show.
   The game was important.
   The game was against a conference opponent.
   The game was during October.
   **Possible Solution:** The band played on the field during the halftime show of an important October game against a conference opponent.

6. I sat in my seat.
   I did this on one hot day.
   The day was in the summer.
   The summer was in 2010.
   The seat was behind home plate.
   The seat was in Progressive Field.
   The field was in Cleveland, Ohio.
   **Possible Solution:** One hot summer day in 2010, I sat in my seat behind home plate at Progressive Field in Cleveland, Ohio.

## Sentence Construction with Coordinators

**Directions:** "Coordinating conjunctions (*for, and, nor, but, or, yet, so*) join individual words, phrases, and independent clauses. Combine the sentences in each set by coordinating words, phrases, and/or clauses into a single clear sentence. Use any basic conjunctions you think are appropriate. Omit needlessly repeated words, but don't take out important details."

1. The third baseman was not tall.
   The third baseman was not fast.
   The third baseman had a strong arm.
   **Possible Solution:** The third baseman was neither tall nor fast, yet he had a strong arm.

2. The man slipped the ticket into the slot.
   He was happy.
   He wanted the ticket taker to allow him to enter.
   He wanted to enter the ballpark.

**Possible Solution:** The happy man slipped the ticket into the slot, for he wanted the ticket taker to allow him to enter the ballpark.

3. Mom would sit on the front porch.
   Mom would sit in the evening.
   The evenings were warm.
   The evenings were in summer.
   Mom would play her harmonica.
   The harmonica was brass.
   She played happily.
   She played softly.
   **Possible Solution:** Mom would sit on the porch on warm summer evenings, happily playing her brass harmonica softly.

4. Ava may be in the cafeteria.
   Ava may be in the library.
   Ava cannot be in the classroom.
   Her desk is empty.
   **Possible Solution:** Ava may be in the cafeteria or the library, but she cannot be in the classroom, for her desk is empty.

## Sentence Construction with Adjective Clauses

**Directions:** "An adjective clause is a word group that modifies a noun. An adjective clause usually begins with a relative pronoun (such as *who, which,* or *that*) and is a common form of subordination. Combine the sentences in each set into a single clear sentence with at least one adjective clause. Subordinate the information you believe is less important. Omit needlessly repeated words, but don't take out important details."

1. My camera broke after a month.
   My camera was a Nikon.
   It was red.
   It cost over $200.
   **Possible Solutions:**
   My red Nikon camera, which cost over $200, broke after a month.
   Costing over $200, my red Nikon camera broke after a month.
   Breaking after just a month, my red Nikon camera cost over $200.

2. The children attended the circus.
   They were with their class.
   They were in fifth grade.
   They attended Public School 27.

**Possible Solutions:**
The fifth-grade class from Public School 27 attended the circus.
Attending the circus was the fifth-grade class from Public School 27.

3. Mary had a bowling ball.
   The bowling ball was green.
   It weighed 10 pounds.
   It was too heavy for her.
   **Possible Solutions:**
   Weighing 10 pounds, Mary's green ball was too heavy for her.
   Mary's green 10-pound bowling ball was too heavy for her.

4. Nastia Liukin won an Olympic championship in 2008.
   She was the all-around gymnastics champion.
   She was born in Russia.
   She trains in the United States.
   She is coached by her father, Valeri.
   **Possible Solutions:**
   The 2008 Olympic all-around gymnastics champion was Nastia Liukin, a
   Russian-born gymnast who is coached in the United States by her father,
   Valeri.
   Gymnast Nastia Liukin, born in Russia and coached in the United States by her
   father, Valeri, won the 2008 Olympics all-around championship.

## Sentence Construction with Adverb Clauses

**Directions:** "A subordinating conjunction introduces a dependent clause while
indicating the nature of the relationship between one or more independent clauses
and the dependent clause. Combine the sentences in each set by turning the underlined sentence(s) into an adverb clause. Begin the adverb clause with an appropriate
subordinating conjunction. The most common subordinating conjunctions are *after,
although, as, because, before, how, if, once, since, than, that, though, till, until, when, where,
whether,* and *while.* Omit needlessly repeated words, but don't take out important
details."

1. The team put in new seats.
   The seats are in many areas of the park.
   Many more people have come.
   They have come to the games.
   The team is still losing.
   **Possible Solution:** Since the team put in new seats in many areas of the park,
   many more people have come to the games, even though the team is still
   losing.

2. Chloe played her piano.
   The neighbors complained.
   The police came.
   They came to the house.
   **Possible Solution:** Chloe played her piano, although the neighbors complained until the police came to the house.

3. Lauren would kiss her boys.
   She would kiss them on the cheek.
   She kissed them when they wanted her to.
   She kissed them when they did not want her to.
   **Possible Solution:** Lauren would kiss her boys on the cheek, whether they wanted her to or not.

4. Cars are necessary.
   Cars are expensive.
   You must consider the cost of insurance.
   You must consider the cost of maintenance.
   You must consider the cost of gas.
   **Possible Solution:** Although they are necessary, cars are expensive when you consider the cost of insurance, maintenance, and gas.

## Sentence Construction with Appositives

**Directions:** "An appositive is a noun or noun phrase that renames another noun right beside it. The appositive can be a short or long combination of words. Combine the sentences in each set below into a single clear sentence with at least one appositive. Omit needlessly repeated words, but don't take out important details."

1. Marla's bedroom is a disaster.
   It is the biggest disaster area in the house
   Marla's bedroom is full of dirty dishes.
   Marla's bedroom is full of wrinkled clothes.
   Marla's bedroom is full of cat litter.
   **Possible Solution:** Marla's bedroom, the biggest disaster area in the house, is full of dirty dishes, wrinkled clothes, and cat litter.

2. Brian avoided eating the chocolate doughnut.
   Brian is always on a diet.
   **Possible Solution:** Brian, always on a diet, avoided eating the chocolate doughnut.

3. The flying squirrel was a small shape.
   The squirrel was a dark shape.

It flew from tree to tree.

It flew against the evening sky.

**Possible Solution:** The flying squirrel, a small dark shape, flew from tree to tree against the evening sky.

4. William slammed the ball into the basket.

   He slammed it thunderously.

   He was the best player on his basketball team.

   **Possible Solution:** William, the best player on his basketball team, thunderously slammed the ball into the basket.

5. The car pulled up to the curb.

   The car was a long black limousine.

   The curb was in front of the restaurant.

   The restaurant was fancy.

   **Possible Solution:** The car, a long black limousine, pulled up to the curb in front of the fancy restaurant.

6. Charles Schulz died in 2000.

   Charles Schulz died of cancer.

   Charles Schulz was a talented cartoonist.

   Charles Schulz created the *Peanuts* comic strip.

   **Possible Solution:** Charles Schulz, a talented cartoonist who created the *Peanuts* comic strip, died of cancer in 2000.

## Sentence Construction with Participial Phrases

**Directions:** "Participial phrases are short segments of text that can appear at the beginning, middle, or end of a sentence. These participial phrases are almost always set off from the main clause by a comma. The action in a participial phrase should relate clearly to a noun in the main clause. Combine the sentences in each set below into a single clear sentence with a participial phrase. Omit needlessly repeated words, but don't take out important details."

1. Megan reached into her purse.

   Megan was looking for her compact.

   Her compact was round.

   **Possible Solution:** Megan, looking for her round compact, reached into her purse.

2. The cashier glanced at Noelle.

   He was tapping his foot.

   He was annoyed.

   **Possible Solution:** The angry cashier, tapping his foot, glanced at Noelle.

3. Boston is known for its clam chowder.
   Boston is known for the Red Sox.
   Boston is in New England.
   Boston is a great city.
   **Possible Solution:** Boston, known for its clam chowder and the Red Sox, is a
      great New England city.

4. Susan saw a book flying toward her.
   It was a social studies book.
   Susan ducked beneath her desk.
   **Possible Solution:** Ducking beneath her desk, Susan saw a social studies book
      flying toward her.

5. Evelyn was daydreaming.
   She was dreaming of being somewhere other than here.
   She missed the teacher's directions.
   She failed the assignment.
   **Possible Solution:** Evelyn, daydreaming of being somewhere other than here,
      missed the teacher's directions and failed the assignment.

## Sentence Construction with Absolutes

**Directions:** "Absolutes show a special 'how' relationship between two sentences.
The two sentences are combined in a way that subordinates one to the other. Com-
bine the sentences in each set below into a single clear sentence with an absolute.
Omit needlessly repeated words, but don't take out important details."

1. The runner stopped by the park bench.
   He stopped for a minute.
   He ran long distances.
   His skin was covered in sweat.
   **Possible Solution:** The long distance runner stopped for a minute by the park
      bench, his skin covered in sweat.

2. The couple jumped over the puddle.
   They were laughing.
   Their hands were tightly clasped together.
   **Possible Solution:** The laughing couple jumped over the puddle, their hands
      tightly clasped together.

3. George could not finish the cake.
   The cake was chocolate.
   George's stomach was aching.
   **Possible Solution:** His stomach aching, George could not finish the chocolate
      cake.

4. Toby sat on the edge of his bed.
   He sat sleepily.
   His eyes were wide open.
   His head was drooping.
   **Possible Solution:** Toby sat sleepily on the edge of his bed, his eyes wide open and his head drooping.

5. Jada accepted the award.
   It was a science award.
   She had tears streaming down her face.
   Her face was red.
   **Possible Solution:** Jada accepted the science award, tears streaming down her red face.

## Sentence Construction
## with Noun Phrases and Noun Clauses

**Directions:** "A collection of grammatically related words without a subject or without a predicate is called a phrase. Noun phrases are defined as phrases formed by a noun or pronoun and any modifying words. A clause is a collection of grammatically related words including a predicate and a subject (though sometimes the subject is implied). A noun clause is a dependent clause that functions as a noun (that is, as a subject, object, or complement) within a sentence. Like a noun, a noun clause acts as the subject or object of a verb or the object of a preposition, answering the questions 'Who(m)?' or 'What?' Combine the sentences in each set into a single clear sentence with at least one noun phrase or noun clause. Turn all questions (interrogative sentences) into declarative statements. Omit needlessly repeated words, but don't take out important details."

1. What am I wondering?
   How are you getting on with him?
   **Possible Solution:** I am wondering how you are getting on with him.

2. What are the Cleveland fans hoping for?
   They hope that the Indians will win again.
   **Possible Solution:** The Cleveland fans are hoping that the Indians will win again.

3. He feared something.
   He would be unhappy.
   **Possible Solution:** He feared that he would be unhappy.

4. They replied something.
   They would come to the play.
   **Possible Solution:** They replied that they could come to play.

5. Something was a mystery.
   How did the budget pass?
   **Possible Solution:** How the budget passed was something of a mystery.

6. These are Maren's goals.
   The goals are long-term.
   She wants to save money.
   She wants to travel frequently.
   **Possible Solution:** To save money and travel frequently are Maren's long-term
       goals.

In the next chapter, paragraph- and multiple-paragraph-length exercises are provided.

# CHAPTER 15

# Paragraph-Length Exercises

In this chapter, paragraph- and multiple-paragraph-length exercises are provided. Once again, use the samples as exercises in your class, as well as templates for the development of your own paragraph- and whole-discourse-length exercises.

For all of these exercises, you can use the following directions:

> "Combine the sentences in each set into a single clear and interesting sentence. Take out any needless repetition, but leave important ideas. Rearrange the sentences in any way that seems to sound the best to you to form a logically arranged paragraph."

## Exercise 1

**Model Paragraph: *Frankenstein* by Mary Shelley (1818/2003)**

Remember, I am not recording the vision of a madman. The sun does not more certainly shine in the heavens than that which I now affirm is true. Some miracle might have produced it, yet the stages of the discovery were distinct and probable. After days and nights of incredible labor and fatigue, I succeeded in discovering the cause of generation and life; nay, more, I became myself capable of bestowing animation upon lifeless matter.

1. I am not recording a vision.
   The vision is of a madman.
   Remember that.

2. The sun does not more certainly shine.
   It shines in the heavens.
   I now affirm it is true. (than that which)

3. Some miracle produced it.
   The stages of the discovery were distinct. (yet)
   The stages of the discovery were probable.

4. I succeeded in discovering the cause of generation.
   I discovered the cause of life.
   The success was after days of incredible labor and fatigue.
   The success was after nights of incredible labor and fatigue.

5. Nay, more, I became capable of bestowing animation.
   The bestowing was upon lifeless matter. (myself)

# Exercise 2

### Model Paragraph: "The Boscombe Valley Mystery"
### by Sir Arthur Conan Doyle (1891/1986)

The man who entered was a strange and impressive figure. His slow, limping step and bowed shoulders gave the appearance of decrepitude, and yet his hard, deep-lined, craggy features and his enormous limbs showed that he was possessed of unusual strength of body and of character. His tangled beard, grizzled hair, and outstanding, drooping eyebrows combined to give an air of dignity and power to his appearance, but his face was of an ashen white, while his lips and the corners of his nostrils were tinged with a shade of blue. It was clear to me at a glance that he was in the grip of some deadly and chronic disease.

1. The man who entered was a strange figure.
   He was an impressive figure.

2. His step was slow.
   His step was limping.
   His shoulders were bowed.
   These gave the appearance of decrepitude.
   His features were hard.
   His features were deep-lined.
   His features were craggy. (yet)
   His limbs were enormous. (and)
   His limbs showed that he was possessed of unusual strength of body.
   His limbs showed that he was possessed of unusual strength of character.

3. His beard was tangled.
   His hair was grizzled.

His eyebrows were outstanding. (and)
His eyebrows were drooping.
These features combined to give an air of dignity to his appearance.
These features combined to give an air of power to his appearance.
His face was of an ashen white. (but)
His lips were tinged with a shade of blue. (while)
The corners of his nostrils were tinged with a shade of blue. (and)

4. Something was clear to me.
It was clear at a glance.
He was in the grip of some disease. (that)
The disease was deadly.
The disease was chronic.

# Exercise 3

### Model Paragraph: *The Unbearable Lightness of Being*
### by Milan Kundera (1984)

He paid the bills, left the restaurant, and started walking through the streets, his melancholy growing more and more beautiful. He had spent seven years of life with Tereza, and now realized that those years were more attractive in retrospect than they were when he was living them.

1. He paid the bills.
He left the restaurant.
He started walking through the streets. (and)
His melancholy growing more beautiful.
His melancholy growing more beautiful. (and)

2. He had spent years of life.
He had spent them with Tereza.
The years were seven.
He now realized something.
He realized those years were more attractive in retrospect. (that)
They were more attractive than when he was living them.

# Exercise 4

### Model Paragraph: *The Hitchhiker's Guide to the Galaxy*
### by Douglas Adams (1980)

The house stood on a slight rise just on the edge of the village. It stood on its own and looked out over a broad spread of West Country farmland. Not a remarkable house by any means—it was about thirty years old, squattish, squarish, made of brick, and had four windows set in the front of a size and proportion which more or less exactly failed to please the eye.

1.  The house stood on a slight rise.
    The rise was just on the edge of the village.

2.  The house stood on its own.
    The house looked out over a spread of farmland.
    The spread was broad.
    The farmland was West Country.

3.  The house was not remarkable.
    It was not remarkable by any means.
    The house was about thirty years old.
    The house was squattish.
    The house was squarish.
    The house was made of brick.
    The house had windows.
    There were four windows
    The windows were set in the front.
    The windows' size failed to please the eye.
    The windows' proportion failed to please the eye. (which)
    The failing was more or less exact.

# Exercise 5

### Model Paragraph: *Anna Karenina*
### by Leo Tolstoy (1877/1950)

The little girl, her father's favorite, ran up boldly, embraced him, and hung laughingly on his neck, enjoying as she always did the smell of scent that came from his whiskers. At last the little girl kissed his face, which was flushed from his stooping posture and beaming with tenderness, loosed her hands, and was about to run away again, but her father held her back.

1.  The girl ran up.
    The girl was little.
    The girl was her father's favorite.
    The girl ran boldly.
    She embraced him.
    She hung on his neck.
    She hung laughingly.
    She enjoyed the smell of scent.
    She always enjoyed the smell.
    The scent came from his whiskers.

2.  The little girl kissed him.
    She kissed him at last.
    She kissed his face.
    His face was flushed.
    It was flushed from his stooping posture.
    His face beamed.
    It beamed with tenderness.

3.  The girl loosed her hands.
    The girl was about to run away.
    Her father held her back.

# Exercise 6

### Model Paragraph: *Dracula* by Bram Stoker (1897/2000)

When the Count saw my face, his eyes blazed with a sort of demoniac fury, and he suddenly made a grab at my throat. I drew away, and his hand touched the string of beads which held the crucifix. It made an instant change in him, for the fury passed so quickly that I could hardly believe that it was ever there.

1.  The Count saw my face.
    His eyes blazed.
    They blazed with a fury.
    The fury was sort of demoniac.
    He made a grab.
    The grab was sudden.
    The grab was at my throat.

2.  I drew away.
    His hand touched the beads.
    The beads were a string.
    The beads held the crucifix.

3.  It made a change in him.
    The change was instant.
    The fury passed. (for)
    It passed quickly. (so)
    I could hardly believe it was ever there.

# Exercise 7

**Model Paragraph: *A Farewell to Arms* by Ernest Hemingway (1929)**

When I woke I looked around. There was sunlight coming in through the shutters. I saw the big armoire, the bare walls, and two chairs. My legs in the dirty bandages, stuck straight out in the bed. I was careful not to move them. I was thirsty and I reached for the bell and pushed the button. I heard the door open and looked and it was a nurse. She looked young and pretty.

1. I woke.
   I looked around.

2. There was sunlight coming in.
   The sunlight was coming through the shutters.

3. I saw the armoire.
   The armoire was big.
   I saw the walls.
   The walls were bare.
   I saw chairs.
   There were two chairs.

4. My legs were on the bed.
   My legs were in bandages.
   The bandages were dirty.
   My legs stuck straight out.
   I was careful.
   I did not move my legs.

5. I was thirsty.
   I reached.
   I touched the bell.
   I pushed the button.

6. I heard the door.
   The door opened.
   I saw a nurse.
   She looked young.
   She looked pretty.

# Exercise 8

### Grade 6 Model Paragraph: *Wilma Unlimited* by Kathleen Krull (1996)

After years of sitting on the sidelines, Wilma couldn't wait to throw herself into basketball, the game she had most like to watch. She was skinny, but no longer tiny. Her long, long, legs would propel her across the court and through the air, and she knew all the rules and all the moves.

In high school, she led her basketball team to one victory after another. Eventually, she took the team all the way to the Tennessee State Championships. There, to everyone's astonishment, her team lost.

1. Wilma sat on the sidelines.
   She sat for years.
   Wilma couldn't wait to throw herself into basketball.
   Basketball was the game she had most liked to watch.

2. She was skinny.
   She was no longer tiny.

3. Her legs were long.
   Her legs were long.
   They propelled her.
   They propelled her across the court.
   They propelled her through the air.
   She knew all the rules.
   She knew all the moves.

4. She led her team.
   It was a basketball team.
   She led them to victory.
   She led them to one victory after another.
   She was in high school.

5. She took her team all the way.
   She took them to the State Championships.
   It was in the state of Tennessee.
   This happened eventually.

6. Her team lost.
   They lost there.
   They lost to everyone's astonishment.

# Exercise 9

## Grade 5 Model Paragraph: *Beetles, Lightly Toasted*
## by Phyllis Reynolds Naylor (1987)

By the end of April, at least nine fifth graders had broken the boycott and were trying out for the contest. Dora Kray had rigged up some kind of funnel contraption on the roof of the Krays' garage to collect rainwater as a conservation measure. Andy thought this was probably the best idea anyone had thought of so far, until Mother told him that when she was a girl, they always collected water in a rain barrel, and used it to wash their hair. Russ, of course, to conserve land, was still trying to figure out a way to send garbage to outer space, but no one could figure out what Jack was trying to conserve.

1. Fifth graders had broken the boycott.
   Fifth graders were trying out.
   They were trying out for the contest.
   There were at least nine fifth graders.
   It happened by April.
   It was the end of April.

2. Dora Kray had rigged up a contraption.
   It was some kind of funnel contraption.
   It was on the roof of the garage.
   It was the Krays' garage.
   She rigged it to collect rainwater.
   She rigged it as a conservation measure.

3. Andy thought this was an idea.
   Andy thought the idea was the best anyone had thought of so far.
   Andy thought this until his mother talked to him.
   Andy's mother told him that when she was a girl they always collected water.
   They collected it in a rain barrel.
   They used it to wash their hair.

4. Russ was trying to figure out a way to send garbage.
   He was trying to send it to outer space.
   He was trying still.
   Of course he was trying this.
   He was doing this to conserve land.
   No one could figure out what Jack was trying to conserve.

# Exercise 10

**Grade 4 Model Paragraph:** *Orphan Train Rider: One Boy's True Story*
**by Andrea Warren (1996)**

By the end of the week he had begun to relax. He and Leo had spent hours exploring the farm, fishing in the pond, and chasing the chickens and hogs. Mrs. Rodgers had gotten both of them cleaned up, soaking them in the bathtub for a long time. She had washed their clothes and was talking about taking them into town for haircuts. Lee knew he needed one. His hair was so long it hung in his eyes.

1. He had begun to relax.
   It was the end of the week.

2. He had spent hours exploring the farm.
   He had spent hours fishing.
   He was fishing in the pond.
   He had spent hours chasing the chickens.
   He had spent hours chasing the hogs.
   Leo was with him.

3. Mrs. Rodgers had gotten both of them cleaned up.
   She did this by soaking them in the bathtub.
   She soaked them a long time.

4. She had washed their clothes.
   She was talking about taking them into town.
   She wanted to take them into town for haircuts.

5. Lee knew he needed one.
   His hair was long.
   It was so long it hung in his eyes.

# Exercise 11

**Grade 3 Model Paragraph:** *Teammates* **by Peter Golenbock (1990)**

With his head high, Pee Wee walked directly from his shortstop position to where Jackie was playing first base. The taunts and the shouting of the fans were ringing in Pee Wee's ears. it saddened him because he knew it could have been his friends and neighbors. Pee Wee's legs felt heavy, but he knew what he had to do.

As he walked toward Jackie wearing the grey Dodger uniform, he looked into his teammate's bold, pained eyes. The first baseman had done nothing to provoke the hostility except that he sought to be treated as an equal. Jackie was grim with anger. Pee Wee smiled broadly as he reached Jackie. Jackie smiled back.

1. Pee Wee walked.
   He walked directly from his shortstop position.
   He walked to where Jackie was playing first base.
   He walked with his head high.

2. The taunts were ringing.
   The shouting of the fans were ringing.
   They were ringing in Pee Wee's ears.

3. It saddened him.
   He knew it could have been his friends.
   He knew it could have been his neighbors.

4. Pee Wee felt his legs.
   They felt heavy.
   He knew what he had to do.

5. He walked.
   He walked toward Jackie.
   Jackie was wearing the grey uniform.
   It was the Dodger uniform.
   He looked into his teammate's eyes.
   They were bold eyes.
   They were pained eyes.

6. The first baseman had done nothing.
   He had not provoked hostility.
   He sought to be treated as an equal.

7. Jackie was grim.
   He was grim with anger.

8. Pee Wee smiled.
   He smiled broadly.
   He smiled as he reached Jackie.
   Jackie smiled back.

# Exercise 12

### Grade 2 Model Paragraph: "Three Hundred Spartans"
### by Sonia Bradoz (1995)

Leonidas and his Spartans met the Persian soldiers outside the narrow gates. They fought in the wider part of the pass. In time, most of the Spartans had broken their long spears. Then they fought with their short swords, their fists, and their teeth. Such was the bravery of the Spartans. Leonidas was killed in the battle. He showed himself to be the bravest of all. Before the day was over, there were no Spartans left.

1. Leonidas met the soldiers.
   The soldiers were Persian.
   He was with his Spartans.
   He met them outside the gates.
   The gates were narrow.

2. They fought.
   They were in the wider part of the pass.

3. Most Spartans had broken their spears.
   Their spears were long.
   This happened in time.

4. Then they fought.
   They fought with their swords.
   Their swords were short.
   They fought with their fists.
   They fought with their teeth.

5. Such was the bravery.
   The bravery was of the Spartans.

6. Leonidas was killed.
   He was killed in the battle.

7. He showed himself to be brave.
   He was the bravest of all.

8. There were no Spartans left.
   This occurred before the day was over.

# Exercise 13

**Model Paragraph:** *If You Lived in Colonial Times* **by Ann McGovern (1964)**

Sometimes the schoolmaster had more food than he could eat. That happened once to a schoolmaster in the town of Salem. The schoolmaster had too much corn. So he made one of the boys stand near an open window. When the boy saw someone walking by, he tried to trade the extra corn for something the schoolmaster could use.

1. The schoolmaster had food.
   He had food sometimes.
   He had more food than he could eat.

2. That happened once.
   It happened to a schoolmaster.
   It was in the town of Salem.

3. The schoolmaster had corn.
   He had too much.

4. He made one of the boys stand. (so)
   The boy stood near a window.
   The window was open.

5. The boy saw someone.
   He saw someone walking by.
   He tried to trade the corn.
   The corn was extra.
   He tried to trade for something the schoolmaster could use.

# Exercise 14

### Model Paragraph: *Eye Wonder: Earth* by Penelope York (2002)

The Earth's crust is made up of huge plates, which fit together like a jigsaw. The plates have been moving for millions of years and still shift today, with dramatic effects on the shape of our planet's surface. The line that the two plates run along side by side is called a fault. When the plates move against each other, they can create earthquakes, volcanoes, or even mountains.

1. The Earth's crust is made up of plates.
   The plates are huge.
   The plates fit together.
   They fit like a jigsaw.

2. The plates have been moving.
   They have been moving for millions of years.
   They still shift today.
   This has effects.
   The effects are dramatic.
   The effects are on the shape of our planet's surface.

3. The line that the plates run on is called a fault.
   There are two plates.
   They run side by side.

4. When the plates move something happens.
   They can create earthquakes.
   They can create volcanoes.

They can create even mountains.
The plates move against each other.

# Exercise 15

**Model Paragraph: *Eye Wonder: Weather* by Lorrie Mack (2004)**

Rain clouds hold a huge amount of water, which makes them so dense that light can't get through. This is why they look dark and scary. The heaviest rain falls from the biggest, blackest clouds.

1. Rain clouds hold water.
   They hold a huge amount.
   This makes them dense.
   Light can't get through.

2. This is why they look dark.
   This is why they look scary.

3. The rain falls from the clouds.
   The rain is heaviest.
   The clouds are the biggest.
   The clouds are the blackest.

# Exercise 16

**Model Paragraph: *The Other Side* by Jacqueline Woodson (2001)**

It rained a lot that summer. On rainy days that girl sat on the fence in a raincoat. She let herself get all wet and acted like she didn't even care. Sometimes I saw her dancing around in puddles, splashing and laughing.

1. It rained.
   It rained a lot.
   It rained that summer.

2. That girl sat.
   She sat on a fence.
   She sat on rainy days.
   She sat in a raincoat.

3. She let herself get wet.
   She got all wet.
   She acted like she did not care.

4.  I saw her dancing around.
    She was dancing in puddles.
    I saw her splashing.
    I saw her laughing.
    I saw her sometimes.

# Exercise 17

### Model Paragraph: *Lissy's Friends* by Grace Lin (2007)

Because Lissy ate lunch alone, she was finished before lunchtime was over. Since she didn't have anything else to do, Lissy took the lunch menu in front of her and began to fold it. Soon, she had made a little paper crane.

1.  Lissy ate lunch.
    She ate alone.
    She was finished before lunchtime was over.

2.  She did not have anything else to do.
    Lissy took the menu.
    It was a lunch menu.
    It was in front of her.
    She began to fold it.

3.  Soon she had made a crane.
    The crane was paper.
    The crane was little.

# References

Adams, D. (1980). *The hitchhiker's guide to the galaxy*. New York: Harmony Books.

Anderson, P. L. (1982). A preliminary study of syntax in the written expression of learning disabled children. *Journal of Learning Disabilities, 15,* 359–362.

Andolina, C. (1980). Syntactic maturity and vocabulary richness of learning disabled children at four age levels. *Journal of Learning Disabilities, 13,* 27–32.

A perfectly healthy sentence. (n.d.). Retrieved March 15, 2009, from *http://thinkexist.com/ quotation/a_perfectly_healthy_sentence-it_is_true-is/261348.html*.

Applebee, A. (1984). Writing and reasoning. *Review of Educational Research, 54,* 577–596.

Baker, S., Gersten, R., & Graham, S. (2003). Teaching expressive writing to students with learning disabilities: Research-based applications and examples. *Journal of Learning Disabilities, 36,* 109–123.

Beene, L. (1996, March). *Professional writers teaching professional writers: Transcending the borders between professional writers and academic scholars*. Paper presented at the annual meeting of the Conference on College Composition and Communication, Milwaukee, WI.

Bereiter, C., & Scardamalia, M. (1987). *The psychology of written composition*. Hillsdale, NJ: Erlbaum.

Berninger, V. W. (1993). Preventing and remediating writing disabilities: Interdisciplinary frameworks for assessment, consultation, and intervention. *School Psychology Review, 22,* 590–594.

Berninger, V. W., Nagy, W., & Beers, S. (2011). Child writers' construction and reconstruction of single sentences and construction of multi-sentence texts: Contributions of syntax and transcription to translation. *Reading and Writing, 24,* 151–182.

Bradoz, S. (1995). Three hundred Spartans. In C. Bereiter, M. J. Adams, & M. Pressley (Eds.), *Collections for young scholars* (Book 2) (pp. 52–57). Chicago: Open Court.

Brophy, J., & Good. T. L. (1986). Teacher behavior and student achievement. In M. C. Wittrock (Ed.), *Handbook of research on teaching* (3rd ed., pp. 328–375). Upper Saddle River, NJ: Prentice Hall.

Butler, P. (2011). Reconsidering the teaching of style. *English Journal, 100*(4), 77–82.

Cameron, A. (1981). *The stories Julian tells.* New York: Pantheon Books.

Chomsky, N. (1957). *Syntactic structures.* The Hague: Mouton.

Christenson, S. L., Thurlow, M. L., Ysseldyke, J. E., & McVicar, R. (1989). Written language instruction for students with mild handicaps: Is there enough quantity to ensure quality? *Learning Disability Quarterly, 12,* 219–229.

Cooper, C. R. (1973). An outline for writing sentence combining problems. *English Journal, 62,* 96–102.

Crowhurst, M., & Piche, G. L. (1979). Audience and mode of discourse effects on syntactic complexity in writing at two grade levels. *Research in the Teaching of English, 13,* 101–109.

Daiker, D. A., Kerek, A., & Morenberg, M. (1979). Using open sentence combining exercises in the college composition classroom. In D. A. Daiker, A. Kerek, & M. Morenberg (Eds.), *Sentence combining and the teaching of writing* (pp. 160–169). Conway: University of Central Arkansas.

de Beaugrande, R. (1985). Sentence combining and discourse processing: In search of a general theory. In D. A. Daiker, A. Kerek, & M. Morenberg (Eds.), *Sentence combining: A rhetorical perspective* (pp. 61–75). Carbondale: Southern Illinois University Press.

Doyle, A. C. (1986). The Boscombe Valley mystery. In *Sherlock Holmes: The complete novels and stories* (Vol. 1, pp. 306–330). New York: Bantam Dell. (Original work published 1891)

Elbow, P. (1985). The challenge for sentence combining. In D. A. Daiker, A. Kerek, & M. Morenberg (Eds.), *Sentence combining: A rhetorical perspective* (pp. 232–245). Carbondale: Southern Illinois University Press.

Englert, C. S., & Raphael, T. E. (1988). Constructing well-formed prose: Process, structure, and metacognitive knowledge. *Exceptional Children, 55,* 513–520.

Fitzgerald, J., & Stamm, C. (1990). Effects of group conferences on first graders' revision in writing. *Written Communication, 7,* 96–135.

Fitzgerald, J., & Stamm, C. (1992). Variation in conference influence on revision: Two cases. *JRB: A Journal of Literacy, 24,* 21–50.

Frank, M. (1993). *Using sentence-combining to teach sentence structure.* (ERIC Document Reproduction Service No. ED 366 208)

Fuchs, L. S., & Fuchs, D. (2000). Building student capacity to work productively during peer-assisted reading activities. In B. M. Taylor, M. F. Graves, & P. van der Broek (Eds.), *Reading for meaning: Fostering comprehension in the middle grades* (pp. 95–115). New York: Teachers College Press.

Fuchs, D., Fuchs, L., Mathes, P., & Simmons, D. (1997). Peer-assisted learning strategies: Making classrooms more responsive to diversity. *American Educational Research Association, 34,* 174–206.

Gebhardt, R. (1985). Sentence combining in the teaching of the writing process. In D. A. Daiker, A. Kerek, & M. Morenberg (Eds.), *Sentence combining: A rhetorical perspective* (pp. 202–212). Carbondale: Southern Illinois University Press.

Gleason, H. A. (1962). What is English? *College Composition and Communication, 13*(3), 1–10.

Golenbock, P. (1990). *Teammates.* Orlando, FL: Voyager Books.

Graham, S. (1982). Composition research and practice: A unified approach. *Focus on Exceptional Children, 14,* 1–16.

Graham, S. (1997). Executive control in the revising of students with learning and writing difficulties. *Journal of Educational Psychology, 89,* 223–234.

Graham, S. (2006). Strategy instruction and the teaching of writing: A meta-analysis. In C.

A. MacArthur, S. Graham, & J. Fitzgerald (Eds.), *Handbook of writing research* (pp. 187–207). New York: Guilford Press.

Graham, S., & Harris, K. R. (1989). Improving learning disabled students' skills at composing essays: Self-instructional strategy training. *Exceptional Children, 56*, 201–214.

Graham, S., & Harris, K. R. (1997). It can be taught, but it does not develop naturally: Myths and realities in writing instruction. *School Psychology Review, 26*(3), 414–425.

Graham, S., & Harris, K. R. (2004). Writing instruction. In B. Wong (Ed.), *Learning about learning disabilities* (3rd ed., pp. 281–313). San Diego, CA: Elsevier Academic Press.

Graham, S., & Hebert, M. A. (2010). *Writing to read: Evidence for how writing can improve reading. A Carnegie Corporation Time to Act Report.* Washington, DC: Alliance for Excellent Education.

Graham, S., & Perin, D. (2007). A meta-analysis of writing instruction for adolescent students. *Journal of Educational Psychology, 99*(3), 445–476.

Greenwood, C. R., Carta, J. J., & Kamps, D. (1990). Teacher versus peer-mediated instruction: A review of educational advantages and disadvantages. In M. Foot, F. Morgan, & R. Shute (Eds.), *Children helping children* (pp. 177–205). Chichester, UK: Wiley.

Hayes, J., & Flower, L. (1986). Writing research and the writer. *American Psychologist, 41*, 1106–1113.

Hayes, J. R., & Flower, L. S. (1987). On the structure of the writing process. *Topics in Language Disorders, 7*(4), 19–30.

Hemingway, E. (1929). *A farewell to arms.* New York: Scribner's.

Hillocks, G. (1986). *Research on written composition.* Urbana, IL: ERIC Clearinghouse on Reading and Communication Skills.

Hillocks, G. (1987). Synthesis of research on teaching writing. *Educational Leadership, 44*, 71–82.

Houck, C. K., & Billingsley, B. S. (1989). Written expression of students with and without learning disabilities: Differences across the grades. *Journal of Learning Disabilities, 22*, 561–575.

Hugo, V. (1992). *Les misérables* (C. E. Wilbour, trans.). New York: Modern Library. (Original work published 1862)

Hunt, K. W. (1965). *Grammatical structures written at three grade levels* (Research Report No. 3). Champaign, IL: National Council of Teachers of English.

Hunt, K. W. (1979). Anybody can teach English. In D. A. Daiker, A. Kerek, & M. Morenberg (Eds.), *Sentence combining and the teaching of writing. Studies in Contemporary Language #3* (pp. 149–157). Department of English, University of Akron, Akron, Ohio, and the University of Central Arkansas, Conway, Arkansas.

Hunt, K. W. (1983). Sentence combining and the teaching of writing. In M. Martlew (Ed.), *The psychology of written language: Developmental and educational perspectives* (pp. 99–125). New York: Wiley.

Kame'enui, E. J., & Simmons, D. J. (1990). *Designing instructional strategies: The prevention of academic learning problems.* Columbus, OH: Merrill.

Karegianes, M., Pascarella, E., & Pflaum, S. (1980). The effects of peer editing on the writing proficiency of low-achieving tenth grade students. *Journal of Educational Research, 73*, 203–207.

Krull, K. (1996). *Wilma unlimited: How Wilma Rudolph became the world's fastest woman.* San Diego, CA: Harcourt Brace.

Kundera, M. (1984). *The unbearable lightness of being* (M. H. Heim, Trans.). New York: Harper & Row.

Lawlor, J. (1983). Sentence combining: A sequence for instruction. *Elementary School Journal,* *84,* 53–61.

Lin, G. (2007). *Lissy's friends.* New York: Viking.

Lindemann, E. (1995). *A rhetoric for writing teachers.* New York: Oxford University Press.

MacArthur, C. A. (2007). Best practices in teaching evaluation and revision. In S. Graham, C. A. MacArthur, & J. Fitzgerald (Eds.), *Best practices in writing instruction* (pp. 141–162). New York: Guilford Press.

MacArthur, C. A., & Philippakos, S. (2010). Instruction in a strategy for compare–contrat writing. *Exceptional Children, 76,* 438–456.

MacArthur, C. A., Schwartz, S. S., & Graham, S. (1991). Effects of a reciprocal peer revision strategy in special education classrooms. *Learning Disabilities Research and Practice, 6,* 201–210.

Mack, L. (2004). *Eye wonder: Weather.* New York: DK Publishing.

Martlew, M. (1983). *The psychology of written language: Developmental and educational perspectives.* New York: Wiley.

Mason, L. H., & Graham, S. (2008). Writing instruction for adolescents with learning disabilities; Programs of intervention research. *Learning Disabilities Research and Practice, 23*(2), 103–112.

Mathes, P. G., & Fuchs, L. S. (1993). Peer-mediated reading instruction in special education resource rooms. *Learning Disabilities Research and Practice, 8,* 233–243.

McCutchen, D. (1988). Functional automaticity in children's writing: A problem of metacognitive control. *Written Communication, 5,* 306–324.

McGovern, A. (1964). *If you lived in colonial times.* New York: Four Winds Press.

Melvin, M. P. (1983). *The implications of sentence combining for the language arts curriculum.* Paper presented at the National Council of Teachers of English Spring Conference, Seattle, WA. (ERIC Document Reproduction Service No. ED 238 021)

Miller, B. D., & Ney, J. W. (1968). The effect of systematic oral exercises on the writing of fourth-grade students. *Research in the Teaching of English, 2,* 44–61.

Moffett, J. (1968). *Teaching the universe of discourse.* Boston: Houghton Mifflin.

Morenberg, M., & Sommers, J. (2003). *The writer's options: Lessons in style and arrangement* (7th ed.). New York: Longman.

Morris, N. T., & Crump, W. D. (1982). Syntactic and vocabulary development in the written language of learning disabled and non-learning disabled students at four age levels. *Learning Disability Quarterly, 5,* 163–172.

Myklebust, H. R. (1973). *Studies of normal and exceptional children: Vol. 2. Development and disorders of written language.* New York: Grune & Stratton.

Naylor, P. R. (1987). *Beetles, lightly toasted.* New York: Atheneum.

Neman, B. S. (1995). *Teaching students to write.* New York: Oxford University Press.

Neuleib, J., & Fortune, R. (1985). The use of sentence combining in an articulated curriculum. In D. A. Daiker, A. Kerek, & M. Morenberg (Eds.), *Sentence combining: A rhetorical perspective* (pp. 127–137). Carbondale: Southern Illinois University Press.

Newcomer, P. L., & Barenbaum, E. M. (1991). The written composing ability of children with learning disabilities: A review of the literature from 1980 to 1990. *Journal of Learning Disabilities, 24,* 578–593.

Newcomer, P., Nodine, B., & Barenbaum, E. (1988). Teaching writing to exceptional children: Reaction and recommendations. *Exceptional Children, 20,* 559–564.

Ney, J. W. (1981). *Sentence combining: Everything for everybody or something for somebody.* Paper presented at the annual meeting of the Conference on English Education, Anaheim, CA. (ERIC Document Reproduction Service No. ED 199 753)

Nixon, J. G., & Topping, K. J. (2001). Emergent writing: The impact of structured peer interaction. *Educational Psychology, 21,* 41–58.

Nodine, B. F., Barenbaum, E., & Newcomer, P. (1985). Story composition by learning disabled, reading disabled, and normal children. *Learning Disability Quarterly, 8,* 167–179.

Nutter, N., & Safran, I. J. (1983). *Sentence combining and the learning disabled student.* (ERIC Document No. 252-94)

Nutter, N., & Safran, I. J. (1984). Improving writing with sentence combining exercises. *Academic Therapy, 19,* 449–455.

O'Hare, F. (1973). *Sentence combining.* Champaign, IL: National Council of Teachers of English.

Olson, V. L. (1990). The revising processes of sixth-grade writers with and without peer feedback. *Journal of Educational Research, 84,* 22–29.

Perron, J. D. (1974). An exploratory approach to extending the syntactic development of fourth grade students through the use of sentence-combining methods (Doctoral dissertation, Indiana University, 1974). *Dissertation Abstracts International, 35,* 4316A.

Phillips, S. E. (1996). *Sentence combining: A literature review.* (ERIC Document Reproduction Service No. ED 398 589)

Remarque, E. M. (1982). *All quiet on the Western front* (A. W. Wheen, Trans.). New York: Ballantine Books. (Original work published 1929)

Rhodes, L. K., & Dudley-Marlin, C. (1996). *Readers and writers with a difference: A holistic approach to teaching struggling readers and writers.* Portsmouth, NH: Heinemann.

Rockwell, T. (1973). *How to eat fried worms.* New York: Dell.

Saddler, B., & Andrade, H. (2004). The writing rubric: Instructional rubrics can help students become self-regulated writers. *Educational Leadership, 62,* 48–52.

Saddler, B., & Asaro, K. (2008). Beyond noun–verb: The use of sentence combining to improve sentence writing ability. *Insights on Learning Disabilities, 5*(2), 41–50.

Saddler, B., Behforooz, B., & Asaro, K. (2008). The effects of sentence combining instruction on the writing of fourth grade students with learning disabilities. *Journal of Special Education, 42,* 79–90.

Saddler, B., & Graham, S. (2005). The effects of peer-assisted sentence-combining instruction on the writing of more and less skilled young writers. *Journal of Educational Psychology, 97*(1), 43–54.

Scardamalia, M., & Bereiter, C. (1986). Research on written composition. In M. C. Wittrock (Ed.), *Handbook of research on teaching* (3rd ed., pp. 778–803). New York: Macmillan.

Schumaker, J. B., & Deshler, D. D. (2009). Adolescents with learning disabilities as writers: Are we selling them short? *Learning Disabilities Research and Practice, 24*(2), 81–92.

Shelley, M. (2003). *Frankenstein.* New York: Barnes & Noble Classics. (Original work published 1818)

Smith, W. (1981). The potential and problems of sentence combining. *English Journal, 29,* 79–81.

Stoddard, B., & MacArthur, C. A. (1993). A peer editor strategy: Guiding learning disabled students in response and revision. *Research in the Teaching of English, 27*(1), 76–102.

Stoker, B. (2000). *Dracula.* New York: Dover. (Original work published 1897)

Stotski, S. (1975). Sentence combining as a curricular activity: Its effect on written language development and reading comprehension. *Research in the Teaching of English, 9,* 30–71.

Strong, W. (1976). Close-up: Sentence combining. *English Journal, 24,* 56–65.

Strong, W. (1985). How sentence combining works. In D. A. Daiker, A. Kerek, & M. Morenberg (Eds.), *Sentence combining: A rhetorical perspective* (pp. 334–352). Carbondale: Southern Illinois University Press.

Strong, W. (1986). *Creative approaches to sentence combining.* Urbana, IL: ERIC Clearinghouse on Reading and Communication Skills and National Council of Teachers of English.

Strong, W. (1990). *Premises, premises: New ways to think about sentence combining.* Paper presented at the annual meeting of the National Council of Teachers of English, Atlanta, GA. (ERIC Document Reproduction Service No. ED 326 873)

Strunk, W., & White, E. B. (1979). *The elements of style* (3rd ed.). New York: Macmillan.

Tolstoy, L. (1950). *Anna Karenina* (C. Garnett, Trans.). New York: Modern Library. (Original work published 1877)

Troia, G. A. (2006). Writing instruction for students with learning disabilities. In C. A. MacArthur, S. Graham, & J. Fitzgerald (Eds.), *Handbook of writing research* (pp. 324–336). New York: Guilford Press.

Warren, A. (1996). *Orphan train rider: One boy's true story.* Boston: Houghton Mifflin.

Weis, M. (1985). Sentence combining as play: Preparing for insight. In D. A. Daiker, A. Kerek, & M. Morenberg (Eds.), *Sentence combining: A rhetorical perspective* (pp. 213–218). Carbondale: Southern Illinois University Press.

Wilkinson, P. A., & Patty, D. (1993). The effects of sentence combining on the reading comprehension of fourth grade students. *Research in the Teaching of English, 27,* 104–121.

Wong, B. Y. L. (2000). Writing strategies instruction for expository essays for adolescents with and without learning disabilities. *Topics in Language Disorders, 20,* 29–44.

Wong, B. Y. L., Butler, D., Ficzere, S., Corden, M., & Zelmer, J. (1994). Teaching problem learners revision skills and sensitivity to audience through two instructional modes: Student–teacher versus student–student interactive dialogues. *Learning Disabilities Research and Practice, 9,* 78–90.

Wong, B. Y. L., Butler, D. L., Ficzere, S. A., & Kuperis, S. (1996). Teaching low achievers and students with learning disabilities to plan, write, and revise opinion essays. *Journal of Learning Disabilities, 29,* 197–212.

Wong, B. Y. L., Graham, L., Hoskyn, M., & Berman, J. (2008). *The ABCs of learning disabilities* (2nd ed.). Burlington, MA: Elsevier Academic Press.

Wong, B. Y. L., Wong, R., Darlington, D., & Jones, W. (1991). Interactive teaching: An effective way to teach revision skills to adolescents with learning disabilities. *Learning Disabilities Research and Practice, 6,* 117–127.

Woodson, J. (2001). *The other side.* New York: Putnam's.

Yarrow, F., & Topping, K. J. (2001). Collaborative writing: The effects of metacognitive prompting and structured peer interaction. *British Journal of Educational Psychology, 71,* 261–282.

York, P. (2002). *Eye wonder: Earth.* New York: DK Publishing.

Zimmerman, B. J. (1989). A social-cognitive view of self-regulated learning. *Journal of Educational Psychology, 81,* 329–339.

# Index

*f* following a page number indicates a figure; *t* following a page number indicates a table.

## O

Open sentence combining exercises. *see also* Sentence combining/construction exercises
content sources for, 41–48
increasing the complexity in, 39–41
overview, 32–34
transferring to connected writing, 40–41
Oral practice, 57–58. *see also* Practice
Organization, 99–100, 100*f*, 101*f*

## P

Paragraph construction
exercises, 152–165
practice activities and, 100–102
sample unit of instruction, 92–94, 93*f*, 94*f*
whole-discourse exercises and, 35–39
Participial phrases, 108, 133–134, 136–137, 139–140, 148–149. *see also* Grammatical structure
Participles, 108, 134. *see also* Grammatical structure
Part-to-whole learning, 13
Peer conferencing, 62–64, 64
Peer-assisted learning strategies (PALS), 64–65, 84–85, 84*f*, 85*f*, 89–90, 90*f*
Planning, 4, 9–10, 104
Practice. *see also* Independent practice; Scaffolded practice; Sentence combining/construction exercises; Warm-ups
activities for, 97–105
grading and, 67
sample unit of instruction, 81–85, 82*f*, 83*f*, 84*f*, 85*f*, 87–90, 88*f*, 89*f*, 90*f*, 92–94, 92*f*, 93*f*, 94*f*
Predicate, 12
Prepositional phrases, 108, 123, 124–125, 132, 143–144. *see also* Grammatical structure
Prepositions, 121–122
Pronominals, 108. *see also* Grammatical structure
Pronouns, 108, 131–132. *see also* Grammatical structure
Punctuation, 4, 16–17, 68–70
Purpose, phrases and clauses of, 126

## R

Reading fluency, 18
Reason, phrases and clauses of, 124
Relative clauses, 108. *see also* Grammatical structure
Revision
peer conferencing, 63–64
practice activities and, 99
sample unit of instruction, 92–94, 93*f*, 94*f*
sentence combining and, 59–60
syntactic control and, 9–10
Rhythm, 74*f*
Rough drafts, 63–64. *see also* Draft writing; Revision
Run-on sentences, 16

## S

Scaffolded practice, 53–56, 54*t*, 56*t*, 59. *see also* Practice
Sentence combining. *see also* Decombining sentences activities; Practice; Sentence combining/construction exercises; Syntactic control
assessment and, 66–67
basics of, 11–13
benefits of, 15–18, 16*t*
best-practice suggestions, 60–61
cognitive challenge of, 23–26
comparative metrics for the assessment of, 67–74, 69*f*, 72*f*, 74*f*, 75*f*–76*f*
discussion or evaluation of the combination and, 56–57
lists of words useful in, 113*f*–114*f*
metalinguistic awareness and, 18–19
mistakes and, 57
oral practice and, 57–58
versus other types of writing instruction, 19
overview, 11
part-to-whole learning and, 13
peer conferencing and, 63–64
peer-assisted learning strategies and, 64–65
versus "real" writing, 18
sample unit of instruction, 79–96
scheduling practice sessions for, 59
sequence of, 109–115, 111*t*–114*t*
student grouping and, 62–65
teacher role during discussions and, 58–59
teaching sentences and, 49–52
theoretical principles of, 14–15, 14*t*
three segments of sentence-combining lessons, 53–56, 54*t*, 56*t*
writing workshop and, 59–60
Sentence combining/construction exercises. *see also* Practice
with absolute phrases, 149–150
with adjective clauses, 145–146
with adjectives and adverbs, 142–143
with adverb clauses, 146–147
adverb structures, 122–126
with appositives, 147–148
checking for accuracy in, 34–35
content sources for, 41–48
coordinate structures, 116–122
with coordinators, 144–145
cued exercises, 27–32, 30*t*, 39–41
free modifiers, 136–141
grading and, 67
increasing the complexity in, 39–41
noun modifiers, 127–135
with noun phrases and noun clauses, 150–151
noun substitutes, 135–136
open exercises, 32–34, 39–41
overview, 27
paragraph-length exercises, 152–165